LAWS FOR A NATION AND LAWS FOR TRANSNATIONAL COMMERCE

In the 75th Hamlyn Lectures, former Lord Chief Justice of England and Wales Lord Thomas examines Welsh law and the law used for transnational commerce to assess what laws are best national in their application and which are best transnational. He first argues that Wales as a nation should be able to make its own laws on the basis of clear principles and sets out possible solutions to the issues raised by the devolution of law-making powers in 1999.

He then explains the success of English commercial law in attaining transnational use and examines the emergence of transnational law from the late nineteenth century. At a time of unprecedented change and competition, his analysis of the present position of the use of English law for transnational commerce and the challenges it faces provides the essential context for a series of practical options for its continued use in the future.

LORD JOHN THOMAS was Lord Chief Justice of England and Wales from 2013 to 2017. He is President of the Qatar International Court, chairman of the London Financial Markets Law Committee, an international arbitrator and an active member of the House of Lords.

LAWS FOR A NATION AND LAWS FOR TRANSNATIONAL COMMERCE

LORD JOHN THOMAS OF CWMGIEDD

CAMBRIDGE
UNIVERSITY PRESS

CAMBRIDGE
UNIVERSITY PRESS

Shaftesbury Road, Cambridge CB2 8EA, United Kingdom

One Liberty Plaza, 20th Floor, New York, NY 10006, USA

477 Williamstown Road, Port Melbourne, VIC 3207, Australia

314–321, 3rd Floor, Plot 3, Splendor Forum, Jasola District Centre, New Delhi – 110025, India

103 Penang Road, #05–06/07, Visioncrest Commercial, Singapore 238467

Cambridge University Press is part of Cambridge University Press & Assessment, a department of the University of Cambridge.

We share the University's mission to contribute to society through the pursuit of education, learning and research at the highest international levels of excellence.

www.cambridge.org
Information on this title: www.cambridge.org/9781009627832

DOI: 10.1017/9781009627856

First published 2025

A catalogue record for this publication is available from the British Library

A Cataloging-in-Publication data record for this book is available from the Library of Congress

ISBN 978-1-009-62783-2 Hardback

CONTENTS

THE HAMLYN TRUST

The Hamlyn Trust owes its existence today to the will of the late Miss Emma Warburton Hamlyn of Torquay, who died in 1941 at the age of eighty. She came of an old and well-known Devon family. Her father, William Bussell Hamlyn, practised in Torquay as a solicitor and J.P. for many years, and it seems likely that Miss Hamlyn founded the trust in his memory. Emma Hamlyn was a woman of strong character, intelligent and cultured, well-versed in literature, music and art, and a lover of her country. She travelled extensively in Europe and Egypt and apparently took considerable interest in the law and ethnology of the countries and cultures that she visited. An account of Miss Hamlyn by Professor Chantal Stebbings of the University of Exeter may be found, under the title 'The Hamlyn Legacy', in volume 42 of the published lectures.

Miss Hamlyn bequeathed the residue of her estate on trust in terms which it seems were her own. The wording was thought to be vague, and the will was taken to the Chancery Division of the High Court, which in November 1948 approved a scheme for the administration of the trust. Paragraph 3 of the scheme, which follows Miss Hamlyn's own wording, is as follows:

> The object of the charity is the furtherance by lectures or otherwise among the Common People of the United Kingdom of Great Britain and Northern Ireland of the

> knowledge of the Comparative Jurisprudence and Ethnology of the Chief European countries including the United Kingdom, and the circumstances of the growth of such jurisprudence to the Intent that the Common People of the United Kingdom may realise the privileges which in law and custom they enjoy in comparison with other European Peoples and realising and appreciating such privileges may recognise the responsibilities and obligations attaching to them.

The trustees are to include the Vice-Chancellor of the University of Exeter, representatives of the Universities of London, Leeds, Glasgow, Belfast and Wales and persons co-opted. At present there are eight trustees:

From the outset, it was decided that the objects of the trust could be best achieved by means of an annual course of public lectures of outstanding interest and quality by eminent lecturers and by their subsequent publication and distribution to a wider audience. The first of the lectures were delivered by the Rt Hon. Lord Justice Denning (as he then was) in 1949. Since then, there has been an unbroken series of annual lectures published until 2005 by Sweet & Maxwell and from

2006 by Cambridge University Press. A complete list of the Lectures may be found on pages x to xiv. In 2005, the trustees decided to supplement the lectures with an annual Hamlyn Seminar, normally held at the Institute of Advanced Legal Studies in the University of London, to mark the publication of the lectures in printed book form. The trustees have also, from time to time, provided financial support for a variety of projects that, in various ways, have disseminated knowledge or have promoted a wider public understanding of the law.

This, the seventy-fifth series of lectures, was delivered by Lord John Thomas on Thursday 5 October 2023 at Cardiff University, chaired by Professor Lord Carwyn Jones; on Wednesday 1 November 2023, at Birmingham University, chaired by Professor Lisa Webley; and on Tuesday 7 November 2023 at Guildhall, City of London, chaired by Sir David Wootton. The board of trustees would like to record its appreciation to Lord Thomas and also to the three institutions that generously hosted these lectures.

Professor Avrom Sherr
Chair of the Trustees

THE HAMLYN LECTURES

1949	Freedom under the Law by the Rt Hon. Lord Denning
1950	The Inheritance of the Common Law by Richard O'Sullivan
1951	The Rational Strength of English Law by Professor F. H. Lawson
1952	English Law and the Moral Law by Professor A. L. Goodhart
1953	The Queen's Peace by Sir Carleton Kemp Allen
1954	Executive Discretion and Judicial Control by Professor C. J. Hamson
1955	The Proof of Guilt by Professor Glanville Williams
1956	Trial by Jury by the Rt Hon. Lord Devlin
1957	Protection from Power under English Law by the Rt Hon. Lord MacDermott
1958	The Sanctity of Contracts in English Law by Professor Sir David Hughes Parry
1959	Judge and Jurist in the Reign of Victoria by C. H. S. Fifoot
1960	The Common Law in India by M. C. Setalvad
1961	British Justice: The Scottish Contribution by Professor Sir Thomas Smith
1962	Lawyer and Litigant in England by the Rt Hon. Sir Robert Megarry
1963	Crime and the Criminal Law by the Baroness Wootton of Abinger

1964 Law and Lawyers in the United States by Dean Erwin N. Griswold

1965 New Law for a New World? by the Rt Hon. Lord Tangley

1966 Other People's Law by the Rt Hon. Lord Kilbrandon

1967 The Contribution of English Law to South African Law: And the Rule of Law in South Africa by the Hon. O. D. Schreiner

1968 Justice in the Welfare State by Professor H. Street

1969 The British Tradition in Canadian Law by the Hon. Bora Laskin

1970 The English Judge by Henry Cecil

1971 Punishment, Prison and the Public by Professor Sir Rupert Cross

1972 Labour and the Law by Professor Sir Otto Kahn-Freund

1973 Maladministration and Its Remedies by Sir Kenneth Wheare

1974 English Law – the New Dimension by the Rt Hon. Lord Scarman

1975 The Land and the Development; or, The Turmoil and the Torment by Sir Desmond Heap

1976 The National Insurance Commissioners by Sir Robert Micklethwait

1977 The European Communities and the Rule of Law by Lord Mackenzie Stuart

1978 Liberty, Law and Justice by Professor Sir Norman Anderson

1979 Social History and Law Reform by Professor Lord McGregor of Durris

1980 Constitutional Fundamentals by Professor Sir William Wade

1981 Intolerable Inquisition? Reflections on the Law of Tax by Hubert Monroe

1982 The Quest for Security: Employees, Tenants, Wives by Professor Tony Honoré

1983 Hamlyn Revisited: The British Legal System Today by Lord Hailsham of St Marylebone

1984 The Development of Consumer Law and Policy – Bold Spirits and Timorous Souls by Sir Gordon Borrie

1985 Law and Order by Professor Ralf Dahrendorf

1986 The Fabric of English Civil Justice by Sir Jack Jacob

1987 Pragmatism and Theory in English Law by Professor P. S. Atiyah

1988 Justification and Excuse in the Criminal Law by Professor J. C. Smith

1989 Protection of the Public – A New Challenge by the Rt Hon. Lord Justice Woolf

1990 The United Kingdom and Human Rights by Dr Claire Palley

1991 Introducing a European Legal Order by Gordon Slynn

1992 Speech and Respect by Professor Richard Abel

1993 The Administration of Justice by Lord Mackay of Clashfern

1994 Blackstone's Tower: The English Law School by Professor William Twining

1995 From the Test Tube to the Coffin: Choice and Regulation in Private Life by the Hon. Mrs Justice Hale

1996 Turning Points of the Common law by the Rt Hon. the Lord Cooke of Thorndon

1997 Commercial Law in the Next Millennium by Professor Roy Goode

1998 Freedom, Law and Justice by the Rt Hon. Lord Justice Sedley

1999 The State of Justice by Professor Michael Zander QC

2000 Does the United Kingdom Still Have a Constitution? by Professor Anthony King

2001 Human Rights, Serious Crime and Criminal Procedure by Professor Andrew Ashworth QC

2002 Legal Conundrums in our Brave New World by Baroness Kennedy of the Shaws

2003 Judicial Activism by the Hon. Justice Michael Kirby AC CMG

2004 Rights at Work: Global, European and British Perspectives by Sir Bob Hepple QC, FBA

2005 Can Human Rights Survive? by Professor Conor Gearty

2006 The Sovereignty of Law: The European Way by Sir Francis Jacobs KCMG, QC

2007 The Prisoners' Dilemma by Professor Nicola Lacey

2008 Judging Civil Justice by Dame Hazel Genn

2009 Widening Horizons: The Influence of Comparative Law and International Law on Domestic Law by Lord Bingham

2010 Lawyers and the Public Good: Democracy in Action? by Alan Paterson

2011 The Rule of Law and the Measure of Property by Jeremy Waldron

2012 Aspects of Law Reform: An Insider's Perspective by Jack Straw

2013 The Common Law Constitution by Sir John Laws

2014 UK, EU and Global Administrative Law by Paul Craig
2015 A 'Magna Carta' for Children? – Rethinking Children's Rights by Professor Michael Freeman
2016 Fairness in Criminal Justice: Golden Threads and Pragmatic Patches by Dame Sian Elias
2017 Thinking about Statutes: Interpretation, Interaction, Improvement by Professor Andrew Burrows QC
2018 Making Comparisons in Equality Law by Robin Allen
2020 The Great Experiment: Constructing a European Union under the Rule of Law from a Group of Diverse Sovereign States by Eleanor Sharpston QC
2021 Advocacy by Lord Pannick QC
2022 Courts and the Body Politic by Professor Catherine O'Regan
2023 Laws for a Nation and Laws for Transnational Commerce by Lord John Thomas
2024 Frail Professionalism? Lawyers ethics after the Post Office and Other Cases by Professor Richard Moorhead

....

PREFACE TO THE 75TH SERIES OF LECTURES

Over the course of the three lectures given in October and November 2023, which now represent chapters in this book, I look at the relationship between law and nations by considering what laws are best national in their application and what laws are best transnational in their application. One way of considering this is through broad jurisprudential themes or with a very broad and general sweep across vast areas of law. However, in accordance both with Miss Hamlyn's expectation that the lectures should provide explanations of the benefits of law to the ordinary reader and with the request of the Hamlyn trustees to consider speaking on Welsh law and on commercial law in this series of lectures, I have taken these two specific and contrasting fields as a basis for considering the relationship.

The first of these contrasting fields is the law that is needed for and characterises a nation. Law has always been seen as one of the identifying characteristics of a nation. The nature of its law is an important delineating attribute as well as one underpinning governance. Within our isles, Scotland's own law and legal system is one of the characteristics that identify Scotland as a distinct nation.

The second of these fields is law that must take effect transnationally in relation to trade and commerce. Without law to govern transactions between people of different nations, it is not practicable to trade. Although there is a well-developed system for determining which national legal system governs specific dealings between persons of different nations, there has always been a considerable body of law that is common worldwide and systems of law that are widely used. English commercial law has become a pre-eminent system of law widely used in transnational commerce; it has also played a vital role in the development of transnational law besides almost assuming the role of a transnationally used system.

The development of English commercial law and a projection for this millennium were the subject of the 49th series of Hamlyn Lectures given in November and December 1997 by the most distinguished commercial law scholar of our generation, Sir Roy Goode. These were four magisterial lectures that traced the shaping of the common law, the challenges confronting public law and private law in the markets, the relationship between commercial law and equity particularly in the creation of security interests and restitution and views on the international prospects for the next millennium.

Much has happened in a period of just over a quarter of a century since then – the change in the position of the UK in the world's markets, the emergence of digitalisation and AI and the more active promotion of unifying principles and model laws on a transnational basis. Given these changes, it is necessary to examine again the future of English commercial law (as the pre-eminent system of national law used today in transnational commerce), the development of transnational law and the options for English commercial law for the future.

In contrast to the continued growth in the practical need for such transnational law, the last twenty-five years in the UK has seen a growth in the demand for national law. This began with (1) the restoration of a separate executive government and legislature to Scotland, which already had its own judicial system and law, (2) the gradual provision of an executive government and legislature to Wales (though without providing for its own judicial system) and (3) Brexit with the severing of governmental, legislative and judicial powers from those of the European Union. Although Scottish law was the subject of the 13th series of Hamlyn Lectures, although distinguished Welshmen have given lectures in the series and although Lord Bingham gave the first of the 2009 lectures at Dinefwr Castle (long associated with the golden age of Welsh law), neither Wales nor Welsh law have enjoyed more than incidental consideration or a passing reference in the seventy-four prior series of Hamlyn Lectures. There were good reasons for this because, as a distinct system of law, Welsh law was abolished in 1543 and its distinct courts were abolished in 1830.

The initial minimalist restoration of law-making to Wales in 1998 after an interval of over 450 years and the developments in the 25 years since then provided the opportunity to ask in the first lecture by reference to Wales, but in the wider context I have set out, what is the appropriate scope of the laws that should be adopted by or accorded to a nation? The need to explore this question was reinforced (1) by my experience of the development of law-making in Wales from 1998 seen first from my perspective as a judge, then as chair of the Commission to examine whether Wales should have power to make its own criminal and other laws and administer its own justice system, (2) by my engagement as a member of the UK Parliament in the process of change consequent on Brexit to the law of the UK and of its constituent nations and (3) by the other work being done in Wales, including the Independent Commission on the Constitutional Future of Wales chaired by Professor Laura McAllister and the Rt Hon. Dr Rowan Willams, which reported after the lectures had been delivered.[1] In the first lecture, I seek to examine by reference to Wales the rational and pragmatic basis on which nations should determine what laws they require as nations through the exercise of law-making powers; and by law-making, I include the interpretation and development of law by the judiciary.

In the second and third chapters, I go on to examine the needs of international commerce for law, particularly in the light of the significant changes to our world. After explaining those changes, the reasons why English commercial law developed so successfully to meet those needs and the steps being taken to develop a greater scope for transnational law, I set out options for the future for English commercial law.

As a nation's laws are an important delineator of nationhood and the spirit of a nation, it becomes clear, when examining the law a nation should be able to make, that it is principle that should govern the scope of the laws rather than political expediency and the desire to retain political power. The study of Wales seeks to explain why this is so important.

[1] The final Report was published on 18 January 2024; the Commission is referred to as the McAllister/Williams Commission. The Welsh Government responded, welcoming the report in March 2024.

In contrast, in examining the law used for transnational commerce, it becomes clear that it is pragmatism and the use of law to support the interests of a nation rather than principle that has formed the basis on which the law used has evolved.

I have drawn on my experience from my first days as a practitioner over fifty years ago, as a judge in the UK and now in Qatar, as an arbitrator, as a member of the UK Parliament and as an active participant in legal associations that work on a transnational basis, particularly the European Law Institute and the Standing International Forum of Commercial Courts. It is important to emphasise at the outset I am speaking from the perspective of experience gained over the years as a practising lawyer and a judge, not as a politician or an academic.

I have also drawn on my experience over some years of trying in a single lecture to convey to students at the Summer Law School organised by Professor Dr Michael Rainer at the University of Salzburg the spirit of the English common law, its influence and its ability to deal with change at a pace never before experienced. I have also been very fortunate in the assistance and guidance I have received from Professor Thomas Watkin KC, Professor Richard Rawlings, Professor Emyr Lewis, Dylan Hughes, Professor Sir Roy Goode KC, Dr John Sorabji, Brian Gray, Chief Executive of the London Financial Markets Law Committee, and Professor Gerald McMeel KC.

I also wish to express my gratitude to the Hamlyn trustees and in particular Professor Avrom Sherr, its chair, Professor Rebecca Probert of Exeter University, Joshua

Rozenberg KC and Professor Roger Halson. I am also very grateful for their immense kindness and generosity at hosting the lectures in October 2023 at Cardiff to Professor Dave Cowan and Professor Lord Carwyn Jones (of Aberystwyth University), at Birmingham in November 2023 to Professor Lisa Webley and Professor Warren Barr and at Guildhall in the City of London in November 2023 to Sir David Wootton, Chris Hayward, chairman of the Policy and Resources Committee of the City of London and Paul Double CBE, the then City of London Remembrancer.

TABLE OF CASES

1

Laws for a Nation

Wales

The Approach to Laws for a Nation

Before attempting to explain what appears to be the vast and hugely complex subject of the laws that a nation needs that are best for that nation and national in their application as distinct from law that is best for commerce that operates transnationally, it may be helpful to signpost the scope of this first chapter by identifying at the outset the questions to be addressed in turn, using Wales as a case study:

1. Why does a nation need its own law? What are the principles that should govern the scope and extent of that law (omitting at this stage the principle applicable to the position of a nation within a Union)?
2. How was Welsh law developed and then abolished? How in 1999 was law-making restored to the Welsh nation?
3. What assessment can be made twenty-five years after the restoration of law-making to the Welsh nation, given the incredibly complex way it was restored and the changes that have since occurred?
4. What principles should apply to the law-making position of a nation within a Union?
5. What role should the principles play?
6. What are the options for law-making powers for the Welsh nation based on the principles?

1.1 Why Does a Nation Such as Wales Need Its Own Laws? What Are the Principles That Should Govern the Scope and Extent of That Law?

1.1.1 Why Is Law So Important to a Nation?

It may seem superfluous to begin by explaining the centrality to a nation[1] of law and its justice system. However, experience has shown that most take law for granted and do not think about its centrality. Most people, for example, accept the rule of law as if this was something that was clearly understood by all, but which few in reality do.

Law is in fact the foundation necessary for all nations.[2] It establishes and defines the powers of the nation's governance; it regulates the relations between citizens and the state and relations between citizens and other citizens.

[1] Lord Thomas (2017) The Centrality of Justice: Its Contribution to Society and Its Delivery. In *Being a Judge in the Modern World* (ed. Jeremy Cooper), Oxford University Press, page 149 (Based upon Lord Williams of Mostyn Memorial Lecture 10 November 2016).

[2] As it was to earlier forms of society – see Fernanda Pirie (2021) *The Rule of Laws*, Profile Books (Pirie) especially the introduction at pages 3–14. I have taken the 'nation' rather than the 'state' as the basis for this examination, as a nation is the unit of a society with which people more readily identify and status as a state is a concept of international law. A state and a nation both require a people, a territory on which the people are settled and a government. A state is differentiated for the purposes of international law by the requirement that its government must be a sovereign government: see L. F. L. Oppenheim (1992) *International Law*, 9th edition, Longmans, vol. 1 at pages 120–123.

The last is essential for the resolution of disputes and the underpinning of commerce.

Again, some understand a justice system as providing a dispute resolution service. That is a misconception. It is a pillar of a nation's democratic government because the justice system safeguards the rule of law, maintains the certainty of the law, while allowing for its development, provides public access to the law, provides openness and accountability, and ensures that decisions are made independent of interests.[3]

1.1.2 The Needs of a Nation for Its Own and Distinctive Laws

Why then does a nation seek its own and distinctive laws? There is a general consensus that a nation great or small should be free to maintain and develop its distinctive character.[4] That distinctive character and the nation's common values are expressed most clearly though the nation's law. In doing so, it gives the clearest expression to the spirit of a nation.

However, there are laws that are either universal or transnational in their application and from which nations do not and should not diverge. Piracy *iure gentium* (by the law of nations) was amongst the first subjects of such universal law. Today the principal fields of such law are those that relate to individual liberty such as laws that prohibit slavery, arbitrary

[3] As explained more fully in Lord Thomas The Centrality of Justice at pages 153–159.

[4] Sir Reginald Coupland (1954) *Welsh and Scottish Nationalism, a Study*, Collins (Coupland) at page xix.

arrest and punishment and other principles that are embodied in the Universal Charter of Human Rights and regional conventions such as the European Convention on Human Rights. Although there are fundamental laws about which there is, at least in theory, no dispute, the extent and scope of the laws that can be categorised in this way can depend on the nature of the form of government. For example, the extent and scope in liberal democracies is generally much greater than in nations that have more restrictive forms of government.[5]

Transnational law has developed to meet the practical needs of nations, particularly laws that govern trade, finance and commerce, as their needs are best served by laws that are not national but transnational in their application.[6] Although the way this developed is explained in Chapter 2,[7] some examples are necessary. The law of general average, emerging as it did in Rhodes in the third to fourth century BCE is a good example of early and generally applicable transnational commercial law. In the early middle ages, the special characteristics of a bill of lading and of a policy of marine insurance were developed in medieval Europe. It was the genius of English law that developed these further.

[5] See European Law Institute (2024) Charter of *Fundamental Constitutional Principles of a European Democracy* (Rapporteurs Takis Tridimas and Elie Muir).

[6] This was the view taken by Scottish businessmen who supported the UK codifications of the late nineteenth century – see Chapter 2 at page <120> and Lord Hope, *The Role of the Judge in Developing Contract Law* (2011) 15 Jersey and Guernsey Law Review 10.

[7] See Chapter 2 at page <96> and following.

However, there are very many areas of law where the needs of a nation's people are best served by that nation being in a position to make its own laws and making them. The question to address by reference to Wales as a case study are what principles should influence the decision on where that line should be best drawn to benefit the people of a nation.

1.1.3 *Wales as a Nation?*

If Wales is to serve as a case study for nations needing their own distinctive laws, then it is necessary to refer to the question sometimes still raised as to whether Wales truly is a nation.[8] I do not think today anyone doubts that Wales is a nation. However, there have been suggestions that it is not really a nation: a good example is provided by Lord Simon of Glaisdale:[9]

> The Welsh are a nation –in the popular, though not in the legal, sense – by reason of Offa's Dyke, by recollection of battles long ago and pride in the present valour of their regiments, because of musical gifts and religious dissent, because of fortitude in the face of economic adversity, because of the satisfaction of all Wales that Lloyd George became an architect of the welfare state and prime minister of victory.

[8] What constitutes a nation has often been the subject of discussion by many. Professor Sir Reginald Coupland was right when he enumerated the primary elements but stated it defied a precise all-inclusive definition; see Coupland at page xix.

[9] *London Borough of Ealing v Race Relations Board* [1972] A.C. 342 at page 364.

More surprisingly have been contentions that it is not,[10] where reliance has been placed on matters such as the absence of any distinct legal system, lack of a capital city until Cardiff was designated as the capital in 1955 (some had mischievously referred to Liverpool as it was said to have more Welsh people than any other city), its historically indistinct border (highlighted by the ambivalent status of Monmouthshire) and the formidable geographical obstacles to unity.

Although the Aberdare Commission on education in Wales had in 1880 made clear that Wales had a distinct nationality of its own,[11] just under a century later the Kilbrandon Commission had to justify the reason it considered Wales should be treated in the same way as Scotland and given legislative powers. It did so in these terms:

> There remain a strong sense of Welsh identity, a different way of looking at things and a distinct feeling that the needs and interests of people in Wales must be considered separately from those of people elsewhere in the United Kingdom.[12]

10 See some of the citations quoted by Professor Sir David G. T. Williams QC in September 1974 *Wales and Legislative Devolution*, paper delivered at a conference of the UK Committee on Comparative Law, published in *Devolution* (ed. H. Calvert); Professional Books (Sir David Williams 1974 lecture) at pages 89–91; and at (1975) Cambrian Law Review 80; and Professor Sir David G. T. Williams (December 1993) *Wales the Law and the Constitution*, Lord Morris of Borth-y-Gest lecture (Sir David Williams Lord Morris Lecture 1993).

11 *Report of the Committee on Intermediate and Higher Education in Wales*, 1881 at pages 46–47.

12 *Democracy and Devolution Proposals for Scotland and Wales* (Cmnd. 5732) (Kilbrandon Commission) at paragraph 130.

Welsh identity was also often characterised as linguistic and cultural (sometimes itself debunked as spurious) rather than political and legal. Although this was based on ignorance of the major events in the history of Wales, the laws and justice system Wales had enjoyed and the contribution Wales had made to legal development and the absence (in modern times) of its own law and legal system was a principal reason used to justify the different treatment of Wales to Scotland at the end of the twentieth century.[13]

Thus, a nation's ability to make its own laws through its own legislature and to develop and interpret those laws through its own judiciary is a significant factor in differentiating a nation and in strengthening it. The scope of the laws a nation should be able to make must, however, be based on principles.

1.1.4 *Principles That Govern Choice of Law for a Nation*

1.1.4.1 First Principle: The Values and Ambitions of a Nation

The first principle is that a nation should be able to make laws that will foster and support the kind of society that it aspires

[13] As Professor Sir David G. T. Williams QC pointed out in 2000: *Wales, the Law and the Constitution*, Inaugural lecture of the Centre for Welsh Legal Affairs at Aberystwyth University (31 Cambrian Law Review 51) (Sir David Williams Inaugural Lecture 2000):

> A fuller appreciation of that history might have avoided the adoption of executive as opposed to legislative devolution, for executive devolution maintains a strong and visible comprehensive control from Westminster and Whitehall while at the same time effectively reducing direct Welsh influence in Westminster and Whitehall.

to establish, its tolerance of views and conduct that are permitted, the family or other unit it wishes to strengthen, the nature of its education system, the extent of the health care it provides or the extent to which it wishes to enhance privacy. Although across most nations certain types of conduct are generally criminalised, a nation is entitled to determine whether there is conduct that should be permitted such as assisted dying or the extent of the criminalisation of drugs. The type and severity of punishment of criminals is again a matter that is for a nation to decide in the same way as it should decide on the type of policing it considers best meets its needs.[14]

The laws will also set the criteria for social and economic support, economic development and the transmission of wealth between generations. It will set the degree of protection consumers require, the circumstances in which compensation must be paid and the nature of the remedies available.

The values will change over time. For example, if (as I will outline) the ambitions of those who at the turn of the nineteenth and twentieth centuries sought for Wales its own executive government, legislature and judiciary had succeeded, there is no doubt that the relationship of the church and chapels and the rights in respect of land would have been considered so important that Wales would have ensured laws in respect of these were made as a matter of priority.

[14] Excellent illustrations of the need are provided in D. Newman and R. Dehaghani (2022) *Experiences of Criminal Justice: Perspectives from Wales on a System in Crisis*, Bristol University Press.

1.1.4.2 Second Principle: The Distinct Culture and Language of a Nation

A second principle is law that is needed to protect or strengthen the culture of the people of the nation. In relation to Wales, of primary importance has been law that protects and promotes the Welsh language, education, its cultural heritage and its modern culture. It can, if it wishes, as Wales has done, protect Welsh by legislating in Welsh and giving it an equal status to English.

This was seen by the six members of the Kilbrandon Commission who in 1973 favoured 'a generous measure of devolution'[15] as required for Wales as a nation:

> A distinctive community with its own needs and interests and with a culture and language to preserve and foster, and there is scope for a substantial volume of separate legislation devised by the Welsh people to meet those special needs. Those of us who take this view believe that a generous measure of devolution, in recognition of the national identity of Wales and as a counter to the growing scale of government and spread of uniformity, would be more likely to strengthen than to weaken the unity of the United Kingdom.

1.1.4.3 Third Principle: The Capacity, Resources and Experience to Make and Develop Law

A third principle is the capacity and resources available to make law and develop that law. Sometimes it is asserted a

[15] Paragraph 1152.

nation should only have limited powers to make and develop law on the basis that the nation or the state does not have the experience to make its own law and to govern. This is the usual argument of nations who wish to exercise dominance over other nations or those who do not wish to see a nation have more than the minimum of its own distinct law.

It is, however, not a principle that should be determinative of the scope of the law that a nation should be entitled to make. Making any law entails costs, skills and resources, and a nation must be capable of achieving these. However, there are two courses that can be adopted while capacity and resources are developed. First, when a nation obtains its own powers of government, it is usual for the nation at first to adopt the law that had hitherto applied in the nation and make changes to that adopted law as experience and capacity develop. The choice as to what to keep or what to change is for the nation. Second, a small nation may need to prioritise work on certain areas of the law; if it does not have sufficient resource or skills available to craft its own distinct law, it may borrow the text of some laws from other states. Therefore, although capacity and resources are essential, these can be developed and should not be used to deny a nation its own choice of law.

The further development and interpretation of the nation's law should be made by those who live in and actively participate in the life of the nation. This is not something that can be outsourced to a judiciary that is not an integral part of the three branches of government within the nation; that is because such interpretation and development requires an understanding of the nation, its own distinctive characteristics, its governance, its polity and the circumstances in which the laws have been made. Such capacity has to be fostered as does the necessary support from a legal profession, which, though practising as widely as other jurisdictions permit, sees as its primary objective serving the needs and developing the laws of the nation.

1.1.4.4 Fourth Principle: The Making and Administration of Simpler and Accessible laws

A fourth principle is the vision and will of a nation to make law as simple and as accessible as possible and as well as being as straightforward as possible to administer. This is essential if law is to play its proper role for a nation in meeting the needs of that nation.

The simplicity of law depends largely on:

a. The skill of the makers of the law, whether the maker is a legislator or a judge, in expressing it shortly and clearly.
b. The willingness of the maker of the law to trust the person who is going to carry it out or administer it. Detailed and complex codes or regulations in such diverse fields as police conduct, the administration of social security and sentencing of offenders often reflect the need to control the application of the law and to try and achieve its consistent application. In a small nation, it is often sufficient to rely on knowledge of and trust in those who are to administer the law rather than imposing constraints on discretion.
c. The willingness of the maker of the law to systematise or codify it. UK legislation is an example of unsystematised legislation and of a reluctance to codify or restate the law,

an issue relevant to English commercial law addressed in Chapter 3.[16] Wales is taking a different course as I will shortly explain.[17]

d. The method of drafting and interpreting. Some speak of the difference between the common law method of interpreting law by an examination of the language employed and of the civilian method of interpreting by reference to general principles and guidance. Each nation should have a choice, which often relates to the legislature's trust in the independence, ability and understanding of its judiciary.

If a nation is to make its own distinctive law, then it must have the capacity to make that law accessible. This has been recognised to be a constraining factor in many nations as assistance is often required in understanding and using legal rights.

Relevant to ease and effectiveness of administration of law and to responsibility and accountability is the coherence and size of the nation. It is well recognised that it is often simpler to achieve effective administration of law in a small nation and to hold to account those who have the responsibility for the governance of the nation.[18]

[16] See Chapter 3 at pages <174> and following.

[17] See Chapter 1 page <34>.

[18] Sometimes reference is made to localism and subsidiarity, but these terms may not be apt as they may distract from examining the issues from the perspective of a nation. In the case of a small nation, the size and demography of a nation achieves the same objectives. The terms are, however, relevant to a nation within a Union discussed under the sixth principle, as within a Union of nations having as many decisions as possible made by the nation reflects the principle of subsidiarity.

1.1.4.5 Fifth Principle: The Ability to Address the Concerns of Its People

A fifth principle is the ability to address through law the concerns of its people. The failure by those who govern or who make or interpret the law to understand the concerns of the people (or the perception of such failure) inevitably leads to discontent and unrest. It is much easier to understand and address such concerns if the people of a nation has its own government and its own law-making powers. The laws can then be drafted and interpreted in such a way as to meet those concerns.

1.1.4.6 Sixth Principle for a Nation within a Union

There is a sixth and key principle for a nation that is part of a Union, namely, achieving the right balance between the respective powers of the Union to make law for the Union and the powers of the nation within the Union to make law for the nation. To address that balance, context is essential.[19] In Wales that context includes the long history of its law and the way in which law-making was restored in 1999 and thereafter. Furthermore, as a lack of an understanding of the past was an important factor in the minimalist law-making powers granted to Wales and the Welsh nation in 1998,[20] that has to be corrected if Wales is to be treated in the same way as other

[19] As Professor Linda Colley pointed out in 2014, *Acts of Union and Disunion*, Profile Books, at page 147 (Colley), 'to understand the current divisions and debates (and much else) we need to take careful note of the past. It is history, more than geography, that accounts for the current situation in the United Kingdom'.

[20] See Sir David Williams Inaugural lecture 2000.

nations; there is no basis for what is described as Welsh exceptionalism. I will consider this sixth principle under the fourth of my questions but only after I have explained the context of Wales and the Welsh nation as a case study.

1.2 Wales as a Case Study: How Was Welsh Law Developed and Then Abolished? How in 1999 Was Law-making Restored to the Welsh Nation?

1.2.1 The Background to the Use of the Welsh Nation as a Case Study

Although the events before 1999 are fairly straightforward, the events thereafter are complex and involve highly technical issues. A word about the approach taken to using Wales and the Welsh nation is therefore necessary:

1. Since the initial restoration of law-making powers to Wales, there has been much concentration on the practical. The Commission on Justice for Wales, for example, examined the question of whether Wales should have control of its own justice system by approaching the issue with an emphasis on the practical and pragmatic. It concluded after a detailed review set out in a report of some five hundred pages that there was a strong case that Wales should have its own justice system.[21]

[21] *Justice in Wales for the People of Wales*, October 2019, www.gov.wales/sites/default/files/publications/2019-10/Justice%20Commission%20ENG%20DIGITAL_2.pdf.

2. Although this chapter encompasses practicalities, including those in relation to justice, its focus is on the principles applicable to the much wider question of the needs of a nation and its spirit. Those needs can only be met if the nation has a governmental structure to make such laws. In modern times, the governmental structure of a nation is best examined through the generally accepted principle that the powers and responsibilities of a nation are shared between three branches of government – the executive (commonly called the government), the legislative (the parliament) and the judicial (the courts), each being independent of the other but also being interdependent on each other.[22] In taking Wales as a case study, the way Wales gradually acquired powers of government over the last twenty-five years is central to consideration of the issue as to the laws Wales as a nation ought to be able to make. To make this highly complex subject more 'digestible', this chapter focuses on these universally accepted core components of government and law-making. That is an easier course than examining the minutiae of the evolution of governmental powers over twenty-five years or reviewing the enormous volume of material[23] that exists on the issue, even if this is confined to Wales alone.

[22] See Lord Thomas (15 June 2017) *The Judiciary within the State – the Interrelationship between the Branches of the State*, Michael Ryle Memorial Lecture given at the Palace of Westminster, www.judiciary.uk/wp-content/uploads/2022/07/lcj-michael-ryle-memorial-lecture-20170616.pdf.

[23] This is an invaluable resource, though usually directed at those who are immersed in law or the theory and practice of government and politics.

3. Where a nation is part of a Union, as Wales is, the extent of the laws it should make for itself also depends on the laws that the Union should make – itself a question that involves consideration of the purpose and nature of the Union and the powers allocated to it.
4. The position of the Union can be examined either by considering what should be conferred (or in the terminology commonly employed in the UK 'devolved') by the Union on its constituent nations or by considering what laws the nations of the Union ought to be able to make and those which it is for the Union to make. Looked on in the second way, the key considerations are (1) the purpose of the Union and (2) the governmental arrangements of the Union for the joint exercise of powers where joint exercise is necessary. Greater focus is therefore needed on the laws a nation needs and the extent to which it should pool some laws with the Union or accept that some laws should be transnational.
5. As it is important to draw a distinction between a nation and other entities within a nation such as a region or cities (such as London or Manchester), the application of the term 'devolution' to both the allocation of powers to Scotland, Wales and Northern Ireland and the allocation of powers to entities within England (as is done in the Levelling Up and Regeneration Act 2023) can add confusion. 'Devolution' is an appropriate word where it is used historically, but it is better now to speak of the allocation of the powers of the executive, legislative and judicial branches of government to nations and to a Union rather than to use the term devolution.

1.2.2 *The Development, Life and Abolition of Laws for the Welsh Nation*

The history of the law that developed and prospered for the Welsh nation culminating in about 945 with the Code of Hywel Dda is today much better known in Wales from its coverage in mainstream works.[24] It is only therefore necessary to mention seven points about early Welsh law to provide the relevant historical context:

- First, the law was Welsh law and administered by Welsh judges. The law was significantly different from the law in England of that time but at least on a par with it and the law of the other nations of Europe.
- Second, It was a well-developed and sophisticated system, covering law, procedure, judges[25] and administration.[26]
- Third, it was codified.
- Fourth, Welsh was the language of the law and Welsh developed its own legal terminology as a natural part of its language.
- Fifth, the laws of Wales adapted over the centuries by applying its principles to meet new situations.
- Sixth, it can be rightly said that the law provided an identity and focus of unity for the people of Wales and defined its

[24] Such as R. R. Davies (2000) *Conquest, Co-existence and Change 1063–1415*, Oxford University Press (R. R. Davies); Thomas Glyn Watkin (2012), *The Legal History of Wales*, 2nd ed., University of Wales Press (Watkin).

[25] The laws set out very stringent requirements for judges; see book III – *The Justices' Test Book.*

[26] See the description in chapter 3 of Watkin.

people as a nation.[27] Indeed, from that perspective it could be seen as a golden age to which the people of Wales could look back.[28]

- Seventh, in those parts of Wales later conquered by the Normans and the English, the law adapted in more complex ways.[29] For example, certain aspects of the law relating to the family and inheritance depended on the nationality of the person – English law applying to the English and Welsh law to the Welsh – a system similar to that which today applies in some states. In boroughs, trading customs were adopted from communities with which they were directly or indirectly associated, giving it a rudimentary transnational aspect.

The Acts of Union of 1535 and 1542 unified England and Wales and applied English law to the whole of Wales. Welsh law and customs (particularly the laws of inheritance)[30]

[27] See R. R. Davies at page 19. That identity can also be seen in the attempts of Gerald of Wales (Geraldus Cambrensis, 1146–1223) to establish for Wales a Metropolitan Church at St David's as the seat of an Archbishop of Wales independent of Canterbury; see Professor Norman Doe (2024) *Thrice to Rome* (unpublished play).

[28] See, for example, the introduction to Dafydd Jenkins (1986) *Laws of Hywel Dda* Gomer at page xxxvi.

[29] The Statute of Wales 1284 (a charter made after the conquest of part of Wales by Edward I, which followed a commission appointed to examine the laws used in Wales) permitted most aspects of civil law to continue to be governed by Welsh law – see Judge Ivor Bowen (1908) *The Statutes of Wales*, T. F. Unwin (Bowen) at pages xxix–xl.

[30] S.2 of 27 Henry VIII c.26 'An Act for Justice and Laws to administered in Wales in like form as it is in this Realm' and ss.91–93 and 101 and 128 of 34–35 Henry VIII c.26.

ceased to have effect and English law took its place.[31] English was made the language of the courts and it came to be believed that the use of Welsh was not permitted. A new court system and in particular the Courts of Great Sessions was created for Wales. This system lasted nearly 300 years until 1830 when its abolition completed the absorption of Wales into the legal system of England. Just as Wales became a centre of the industrial revolution, Wales ceased to be a nation that had its own law as a defining characteristic; there was nothing that differentiated it from the law of England.

The abolition of the Welsh courts by the UK Parliament occurred despite the strong revival of Welsh nationhood in the eighteenth and nineteenth centuries particularly characterised in education (such as the eighteenth-century circulating schools), religion (with non-conformity), Welsh culture, and literature. Nonetheless, the completion of the extinction of Wales' legal identity coincided with some English nineteenth-century views of Wales, characterised in terms of the *Encyclopaedia Britannica* entry 'Wales see England'[32]

[31] In the introduction to Bowen, the author mentioned at pages cxxiv–cxxvii *Attorney General v Jones* (1862) LJ Exch 249 (1863) 2 H & C 347 and *Bunbury v Hewson* (1849) 3 Exch 558 which raised questions about the survival of Welsh law and custom. He commented on the first case: 'The important point [the application of the law of Hywell Dda to the seashore in Anglesey, Caernarfon and Merioneth] remained undecided and is left open for further argument by some patriotic litigant.'

[32] 20 George II c.42 (The Wales and Berwick on Tweed Act 1746) provided in s.3 that where England was mentioned in an Act of Parliament, it should be deemed to include 'the Dominion of Wales' and Berwick upon Tweed.

and the attempts to supress the Welsh language, justified in one report on the basis that:[33]

> The evil of the Welsh language is obviously and fearfully great . . .. It distorts the truth, favours fraud and abets perjury.[34]

1.2.3 *The Changes and Ambitions in the Nineteenth and Early Twentieth Century*

However, this total extinction by the first part of the nineteenth century of Welsh law and Welsh courts as a defining characteristic of Wales was only for a very short period, as the later part of that century and the beginning of the next saw marked change.

First, there was the passing by the UK Parliament of three pieces of distinct general legislation that applied solely to Wales,[35] thereby beginning to acknowledge that Wales as a

[33] (1847) *Report of the Commissioners of Inquiry into the State of Education in Wales*, Accounts and Papers 1847, vol. 27, part ii, 66.

[34] The ways in which the commissioners expressed their views had a counter effect, Coupland at 185–195.

[35] See Bowen at pages at cxi–cxiii. At first, such legislation related to the Church and turnpikes. In 1881, the sale of alcohol was prohibited by the Sunday Closing Act 1881 (passed at the instance of the majority of the Parliamentary representatives for Wales). In 1889, the Welsh Intermediate Education Act was passed establishing joint education committees in every county; the Cross Commission had already in 1888 recommended the teaching of Welsh as a specific subject like English (C 5485). In 1902, the University of Wales Act was passed. In addition, there was one important Act in relation to the Church – in 1914, after many failed attempts, the Parliament Act 1911 was used to

nation needed its own laws. Prior to that the only major distinct piece of legislation was the 1563 Act, which provided for the translation of the Bible and Divine Service into Welsh.[36]

Second were the attempts to establish Welsh institutions of government, including a legislature that would make law and courts that would interpret and administer that law for Wales.[37] The aspiration, although attracting only very small support, was considerable as manifested in 'the home rule all round' theme of some of the political demands and accompanied by books by eminent professors and lawyers that sought to give a popular history of Wales as a nation.[38] There was a particular wish to reform law relating to land in Wales,[39] to reform the law that made the Church of England

enact the Welsh Church Act 1914, which provided for the disestablished the Church of England in Wales. This came into effect in 1920 after the First World War.

[36] 5 Elizabeth c.28. See Bowen at pages lxxxiv–lxxxvii who dates it as 1562.

[37] The high point was the report on the *Conference on Devolution: The Speaker's letter to the Prime Minister* (27 April 1921) (Cmd. 692). Many of the details relevant to the law and to the courts are set out Lord Thomas' 2000 Lord Morris of Borth y Gest lecture, *Legal Wales Its Modern Origins and Its Role after Devolution: National Identity the Welsh Language and Parochialism* (2001) 1 Welsh Legal History Society 113; see also Coupland at pages 226–241.

[38] For example, Professor John Rhys and Sir David Brynmor-Jones (QC MP) (1900) *The Welsh People*; T. Fisher Unwin, Sir O. M. Edward (1902) *A Short History of Wales* in T. Fisher Unwin's Story of the Nations series.

[39] Driven by the Royal Commission on Land in Wales and Monmouthshire – see Kenneth O. Morgan (1980) *Wales in British Politics 1868–1922*, Oxford University Press (K. O. Morgan) at pages

the established church, to amend the law so as to permit Welsh to be used in the courts[40] and to create a distinct system of courts for Wales. These changes coincided with and reflected the strengthening of the revival of cultural and other interests in Wales as a distinct nation.

In the speeches, actions and writings of those who sought the rebirth of Welsh law and Welsh courts, the history of Welsh law was important. It was the base of an ambitious vision driven by the existence of the native Welsh laws but also by memories (through rose-tinted glass) of the Courts of Great Session as W. Llewellyn Williams KC[41] pointed out:[42]

> When the old system of the Welsh courts, so cheap and expeditious, is remembered it may be doubted if Wales would not have fared better if our historical judicature had been reformed of its defects instead of being abolished in order that a more cumbrous, costly and technical system might take its place. The simplification of pleadings and procedure during the last 42 years has been a notable feature of legal reform, but the attempt made in 1873 to amalgamate law and equity is largely failed and even the procedure in our commercial courts, direct and non-technical as it is, fall short of the simplicity of the old *conecesse solvere*.

127–129. Among the reforms suggested were security of tenure, compensation for improvements and rents fixed by a land court.

40 Although English was the language of the courts, many of the witnesses were permitted to speak in Welsh and the officers of the court were conversant with Welsh.

41 A liberal MP, leader of the South Wales Circuit and Recorder of Cardiff 1915–1922.

42 July 1911 paper delivered to the Cymmrodorion.

Important also was the emphasis on the use of Welsh in the courts in Wales. Indeed, it is hard to underestimate the profound importance of the survival of the Welsh language to the maintenance of the distinctive identity of Wales. The contrast with Brittany is instructive as Brittany was amalgamated with France in 1529–1535 after the marriage of King Francois I of France and Claude Duchess of Brittany. Its distinctive identity has very largely diminished.[43]

Ambitious and far-sighted though this vision for Wales was, it is important to contrast it with the attitude taken to commercial law at a time when Cardiff was one of the greatest ports of the world, Wales a significant industrial economy and there was much legal business in Cardiff. Although in common with the great English cities of Liverpool, Birmingham and Manchester much commercial litigation was heard on Assize in Cardiff,[44] nothing was sought in relation to the establishment of a court for commercial cases in Cardiff.

[43] See the lectures delivered in the 2005 Colloquium in Cardiff printed in (2006) 6 Welsh Legal History Society 1–234.

[44] The surviving records are poor. Commercial cases can be seen in 1863 when disputes over shipbrokers commission, bills of exchange and carriage of goods were listed or tried at the Glamorgan Assizes. The work grew. In the summer assizes of 1871, three out of the eight effective trials were for breaches of charterparty. By 1880, Glamorgan Assizes had a number of commercial cases – sale of goods, contract disputes between industrial enterprises, disputes over bills of exchange and banking, claims under guarantees, actions for freight, disputes over the demurrage, other claims under charterparties, claims for general average and calls by mutual insurance companies.

With the establishment of the Commercial Court in London in 1895, all the commercial litigation moved to London.[45] If there had been a separate jurisdiction with Welsh courts, it is likely that Cardiff would have developed as a venue for the hearing of disputes given the concentration of the shipping and coal industries. After all, the magnificent civic court building has on its pediment 'Commerce and Industry' reflecting the vision of the early twentieth century for disputes to be heard there.[46] However, there can be little doubt that the disputes would have been determined under English commercial law as that would have been in the interests of Wales to use – the theme of Chapters 2 and 3 in relation to transnational commercial law.

1.2.4 *The Stages of Rebirth in the Twentieth Century*

The ambitious vision for the restoration of law-making powers to Wales was that of a small minority.[47] It died shortly after the end of the First World War.[48] The restoration of

[45] After 1896 it seems only three further shipping cases were listed in the calendar of the Glamorgan Assizes; two were transferred to London. The third case listed was in 1912, but it settled.

[46] It is now only used for the criminal business of the courts.

[47] K. O. Morgan 291–293.

[48] In the years that followed, there was intermittent activity. In Colley, Professor Linda Colley ascribes the moves for institutions and home rule in the nineteenth and early twentieth centuries to a prolonged period of peace and to the shelving of these demands until the 1970s to the effects of war and pride in victory.

some of the powers of government to Wales over seventy-five years later occurred in very different circumstances.

There are three salient events to note about that restoration – the creation of an executive for Wales as part of the UK government in 1964, the transfer of executive power to the National Assembly for Wales in 1999 and the transfer of legislative powers in 2007 and 2011.

1.2.4.1 The Creation of an Executive for Wales as Part of the UK Government

Although during the remainder of the twentieth century there were renewed campaigns for Welsh institutions, it was the creation of the post of Secretary of State in 1964 that recognised Wales as a distinct nation in terms of the executive branch of government. This was a battle fought against the political and civil service establishment in London by Jim Griffiths MP, who became the first Secretary of State for Wales.[49] Lord Morris of Aberavon, one of the progenitors of the restoration of government to Wales, rightly saw this as a key development.[50]

> The setting up of the Welsh office with executive powers, all be it limited . . . was, in my view the keystone to the modern development of Welsh political institutions. The Whitehall mandarins were determined to crib, cabin, and confine him. The Permanent Secretary at the Ministry of

[49] Lord Ted Rowlands (2004) *Whitehall's Last Stand: The Establishment of the Welsh Office, 1964*, Contemporary Wales, vol. 16, 39–52.

[50] Lord Merlyn-Ress 2002 Lecture at the University of South Wales, *The Development of Welsh Political Institutions over 59 Years.*

> Housing and Local Government offered him an office in that department . . .. It was not to be a functional ministry. Jim Griffiths rejected this . . .. He assumed responsibility for housing and local government road transport and certain aspects of local planning. By insisting on being, albeit in a minimal way, a functional minister, he paved the path for the future. Had he not done so, and his successors of both major parties added to the powers of the Welsh Office over the years, there would have been no parcels of power to devolve from the Welsh office to a National Assembly for Wales.

1.2.4.2 The Transfer of the Executive Power to the National Assembly for Wales in 1999

In 1973 the Report of the Royal Commission on the Constitution chaired by Lord Kilbrandon[51] put forward separate schemes for the government of Wales, Scotland, Northern Ireland and the English regions. The types of possible schemes considered ranged from what was termed 'Legislative Devolution' (with powers to legislate granted in specific fields to a directly elected Assembly) to a Council, which was merely advisory.[52] Legislative Devolution would have given the law-making power of the UK Parliament in various fields to a Welsh Assembly with Welsh ministers and a Welsh civil service.

[51] Cmd 5460. It was established by the Labour Government and deliberated for four years between 1969 and 1973.

[52] Federalism was rejected in much the same terms as separatism – paragraph 539.

In recommending the same Legislative Devolution for Wales and Scotland, but not for the English regions, six of the thirteen members of the Commission thought that in the case of Wales Legislative Devolution was justified as it recognised the national identity of Wales,[53] even though it did not then have a separate legal system.

However, in 1975, the Labour Government chose one of the different options, which the Kilbrandon Commission had considered among the possible schemes, namely 'Executive Devolution'.[54] Under this scheme, the executive powers that the Secretary of State for Wales[55] had accumulated since 1964[56] would be transferred to a directly elected Assembly but it would not be given any of the legislative powers of the UK Parliament. The essence of Executive Devolution was that the powers transferred would be those the Secretary of State held as a minister in the

[53] Paragraphs 1150–1152; two more had favoured legislative devolution to Scotland, but not to Wales, on the basis it did not have a separate legal system, had hardly any separate legislation and a less well-defined border.

[54] This had been favoured by only two of the commissioners in the recommendations of the Kilbrandon Commission but was adopted by the Labour Government in September 1974 *Democracy and Devolution Proposals for Scotland and Wales* (Cmnd. 5732).

[55] And by s.10 'power to do anything it considered appropriate to support museums, art galleries, libraries, the Welsh language, the arts, crafts, sport and other cultural and recreative activities'. Powers under s.11 included powers in respect of the war disabled and public passenger transport.

[56] *Our Changing Democracy: Devolution to Scotland and Wales* (November 1975, Cmnd. 6348) turned 'those general principles into detailed proposals' (paragraph 3).

executive government of the UK. The powers were principally administrative – implementing in Wales decisions taken in Westminster or Whitehall. The different treatment of Wales to Scotland (which was to be given Legislative Devolution) was justified by the fact Scotland has its own legal system:[57]

> Taking account of the different structures of law in Scotland and Wales but with the same principles in mind the Government intend that the Welsh assembly should parallel the Scottish counterpart in assuming certain powers of the Secretary of State in respect of delegated legislation.

The limited law-making power to make what is called 'delegated', or 'secondary' or 'subordinate' legislation was simply an aspect of executive power, as ministers in the UK government are given this power by Parliament to make such subordinate legislation within limits set by Parliament in the legislation conferring the power.

Legislation was enacted in 1978 to provide Wales with Executive Devolution. It was made dependent on a referendum in which it was rejected.[58] Although there was considerable discussion about devolution to Scotland in the years between 1978 and 1997, little was done to examine what Wales needed in terms of the three branches of government.[59]

[57] At paragraph 30.

[58] Wales Act 1978. The referendum was held on 1 March 1979 in which 79.7 per cent voted against the proposals.

[59] As Professor Sir David G. T. Williams QC observed on 17 April 1999 in his lecture at the Wales Public Law and Human Rights Association

In 1997, when devolution was offered to Wales, it was the power of the executive branch of government that was offered – Executive Devolution of same type as offered in 1978.[60] Over the years that had elapsed since 1978, the Secretary of State for Wales had accumulated more powers, success depending to a considerable extent on the influence and views of the Secretary of State for Wales[61] and the willingness of Whitehall departments to transfer – the two most determinedly opposed being the Home Office and the Lord Chancellor's Department – now the Ministry of Justice. By 1997, this accumulation had given the Secretary of State for Wales powers over housing, local government, planning, education and training, health, industrial development, roads, tourism, the environment, and agriculture and fisheries. It is hardly surprising, in the light of what had happened in 1978 and the continuing divergent views of the politicians in London and Wales, that 'Executive Devolution' was taken forward (after a referendum where the 'yes' vote was only 50.3

Conference at Cardiff Law School, 'There was relatively little public debate on devolution . . .. In striking contrast to the Constitutional Convention in Scotland from 1989 save for that inspired by bodies such as the institute for Public Policy Research (*The constitution of the United Kingdom*, 1991), and the Constitution Unit based at University College, London (*An Assembly for Wales*, Senedd i Gymru 1996).'

60 *A Voice For Wales, Llais dros Gymru* (22 July 1997) Cm 3718 .

61 For more detail, see Watkin with Greenberg (2018) *Legislating for Wales*, University of Wales Press (Watkin with Greenberg) at pages 19–20. Lord Morris of Aberavon was one of those who was the most active: see his memoir – Lord Morris of Aberavon (2011) *Fifty Years in Politics and the Law*, University of Wales Press at page 109.

per cent) through a complex set of arrangements.[62] The arrangements for transfer of the executive power had three important features:

- As the powers of the Secretary of State that were transferred to the National Assembly were those a member of the executive government had accumulated, they were powers that were intended to be exercised as part of the executive branch of government in cooperation with the cabinet colleagues of the Secretary of State and under the principle of cabinet responsibility. As Professor Richard Rawlings memorably said, 'Wales has a form of government which may safely be described as like nothing else on Earth.'[63]
- These executive powers had been accumulated for the most part at a time of the UK's membership of the EU and therefore large swathes of certain fields were the province of the EU and not the UK government. There was therefore an EU framework, not a UK framework, in which many of the powers could be exercised, particularly in respect of the environment, industrial subsidies and agriculture.

62 Its initial complexity had to take into account that the arrangements were set out in (1) Government of Wales Act 1998 with its 159 sections and 18 schedules, (2) the National Assembly for Wales (Transfer of Functions) Order (1999 S.I. 672) as corrected in 2000 SI 253) and (3) The Memorandum of Understanding and Supplementary Agreements between the UK Government, Scottish Ministers and the Cabinet of the National Assembly for Wales (October 1999) CM 4444.

63 University of Wales O'Donnell Lecture 18 February 2002 at Swansea University – *Towards a Parliament for Wales – Three Faces of the National Assembly of Wales.*

- Although there was no transfer of the powers of the judicial branch of government, there was a tiny transfer of part of what is now seen, but not then seen, as the judicial branch of government. As departmental ministers in the course of their executive functions sponsored the tribunals that were responsible for independent review of administrative decisions by their departments, the Secretary of State for Wales had responsibility for sponsorship of some tribunals that were applicable to the powers he had accumulated. Thus a tiny part of what is now regarded as the judicial branch of the government was transferred.

1.2.4.3 The Transfer of Legislative Power in 2011

It was soon apparent change was needed[64] and change there has been. The initial 'Executive Devolution' has been called 'Phase 1 of Devolution'.[65] In the period to 2017, there were three further phases:

Phase 2 created a legislative branch of government in Wales distinct from the executive and gave it a small degree of power to legislate on matters outside the powers of the

[64] Professor Richard Rawlings (2003) *Delineating Wales: Legal and Constitutional Aspects of National Devolution*, University of Wales Press sets out a detailed analysis of the reasons why this transfer of executive power was just an 'interim stage'. See also Lord Gwilym Prys Davies (August 2000) *The National Assembly: A Year of Laying the Foundations*, Law Lecture at National Eisteddfod of Wales, The Law Society.

[65] The first three phases of Welsh devolution are described in *Agricultural Sector Wages (Wales) Bill* [2014] UKSC 43 at paragraphs 19–29.

executive and within the powers of the UK Parliament, but it could exercise this legislative power only with the consent of the UK Parliament in relation to the matter specified.[66]

Phase 3[67] gave the National Assembly, as the legislative branch of government, more power to make law without having to seek the assent of the UK Parliament, and broadly within the framework of fields that had been transferred as part of the transfer of executive power. The fields on which powers were conferred were listed and the legislative powers confined to what was listed under what is called a 'conferred powers model'.[68]

Phase 4 saw the conferment of powers to raise tax,[69] powers in other fields and a change to the basis on which the National Assembly had legislative powers[70] from a conferred powers model to a 'reserved powers model'. This change appeared to give more powers and brought the

66 Government of Wales Act 2006 following the Richard Commission Report published on 31 March 2004. See Watkin with Greenberg at pages 21–22.

67 Following a referendum in March 2011 required under the Government of Wales Act 2006. The vote in favour was 63.49 per cent.

68 The number of fields in which the National Assembly had powers has often been enumerated as twenty or twenty-one, but for a more accurate identification, see Watkin with Greenberg at pages 81–83.

69 Wales Act 2014.

70 Wales Act 2017. The Commission chaired by Sir Paul Silk (the Silk Commission) in its second report (March 2014) *Empowerment and Responsibility: Legislative Powers to Strengthen Wales* in chapter 4 had favoured a change to a reserved powers model, but the UK government's *Powers for a Purpose: Towards a lasting Devolution Settlement for Wales* (2015) Cm 9020, significantly altered the result.

basis of Legislative Devolution into line with Scotland and Northern Ireland. However, the legislation was drafted in a way that made it open to the interpretation that it actually rolled back the scope of the legislative powers of the National Assembly, though that purpose was strenuously denied by UK ministers.[71]

Since 2017, there has been no single stage of change that could be called Phase 5. Changes have been made in different pieces of legislation, mostly to impose restrictions on the powers held by the Welsh legislature (the Welsh Parliament, which has become known officially as Senedd Cymru [or the Senedd] since 2020) and the Welsh government and the equivalent institutions in Scotland and Northern Ireland, justified as being necessary as consequent on the withdrawal from the EU.

Having outlined these events, I can now turn to the next question – an assessment of the position.

1.3 What Assessment Can Be Made Twenty-five Years after the Restoration of Law-making, Given the Incredibly Complex Way It Was Restored and the Changes That Have since Occurred?

In making an assessment twenty-five years after the initial decision to transfer executive powers and the subsequent

[71] Professor Richard Rawlings in *The Strange Reconstitution of Wales* (2018) Public Law 62, explains the background to the way in which the UK government saw this as an opportunity to reverse the effect of the decision in *Agricultural Sector (Wales) Bill* [2014] UKSC 43 and also the convoluted process by which the Act emerged.

conferral of legislative powers, it is essential first to emphasise how much has been achieved in the making of law for Wales in those twenty-five years. That achievement was comprehensively reviewed by Lord Lloyd-Jones in his magisterial Cymmrodorion lecture in November 2022[72] but in summary:

- There are extensive areas in which the Senedd can exercise legislative power to make law.
- Its powers are recognised to be plenary and as generally, but not always, needing no justification other than the legislation is the will of the legislature.[73]
- Codification (building on a consolidation of legislation) has commenced through the work of the Law Commission and the Welsh government's[74] long-term plans to organise and codify Welsh law.[75] In September 2021, the Welsh government set out its programme to improve Welsh law by consolidation and codification prefaced by a quotation from the Book of Iorwerth:

[72] *The Rebirth of Welsh Law* (November 2022) (2023), vol. 29 Transactions of the Cymmrodorion 95.

[73] *Axa v Lord Advocate* [2011] UKSC 46 at paragraphs 146–147 in respect of the Sottish Parliament but which would seem to apply with equal force to the Senedd; but see *Recovery of Medical Costs for Asbestosis Diseases (Wales) Bill* [2015] UKSC 3 discussed later.

[74] Following on from the Legislation (Wales) Act 2019.

[75] In September 2021 the Welsh government set out its programme (www.gov.wales/the-future-of-welsh-law-accessibility-programme-2021-to-2026-html). The first piece of this consolidation was the Historic Environment (Wales) Act, which received the Royal Assent on 14 June 2023, www.legislation.gov.uk/asc/2023/3/contents/enacted; legislation.gov.uk/asc/2023/3/contents/welsh.

> And by the common counsel and agreement . . . they examined the old laws, and some of them they allowed to continue, others they amended, others they wholly deleted, and others they laid down anew.

- The equality of the English and Welsh languages in legislative drafting is established and implemented through the work of the Office of the Legislative Counsel and systems for agreeing terminology appropriate for the context.[76]
- A significant number of important laws have been passed that reflect the values that the Welsh nation regards as distinctive. Amongst the more important are:
  - the Welsh Language Measure 2011,
  - the Human Transplantation (Wales) Act 2013,
  - the Well-being of Future Generations (Wales) Act 2015,
  - the Social Services and Well-being (Wales) Act 2014,
  - the Violence against Women, Domestic Abuse and Sexual Violence (Wales) Act 2015,
  - the Renting Homes (Wales) Act 2016,
  - the Environment (Wales) Act 2016,
  - the Children (Abolition of Defence of Reasonable Punishment) (Wales) Act 2020,
  - the Curriculum and Assessment (Wales) Act 2021,
  - the Social Partnership and Public Procurement (Wales) Act 2021,

[76] See Watkin with Greenberg; see also Dylan Hughes '*Cyfraith Cymru, Cromwell a'r coronafeirws*' *(Welsh law, Cromwell and the Coronavirus)* (Barn719, Rhagfyr 2022/Ionawr 2023) for an explanation of the work undertaken in the pandemic on regulations that perhaps for the first time led to a widespread appreciation that the law in Wales was different to that in England.

- the Agriculture (Wales) Act 2023 and other legislation taken in respect of the environment (such as a prohibition on single-use plastics) and procurement.
- the Senedd Cymru (Members and Elections) Act 2024

Given the magnitude of the achievement in securing the restoration to Wales of some of its own law-making powers and the immense length of time it took, it was tempting sometimes in the period in and after 1999 to talk up what Wales had obtained. I count myself amongst those who did so,[77] though doing so had some advantages, as the creation of Legal Wales[78] has demonstrated. Moreover, it provided a basis on which it was possible to begin the realisation of the broader ambition to restore law-making through its own proper legislature and a judiciary. It was then neither opportune nor necessary to ask the difficult questions.

However, in noting the achievement, it is necessary to pause and return to the question posed as to whether Wales

[77] I can see the dangers of this in looking again at papers I delivered in 1998 and 1999, particularly (1) at the Conference of UK Judges convened on 9 April 1999 by the Lord Chancellor, Lord Irvine of Lairg – possibly the only such conference ever held – (2) at Wales Public Law and Human Rights Association Conference at Cardiff Law School on 17 April 1999 and (3) in my 2000 Lord Morris of Borth-y-Gest Lecture: *Legal Wales: Its Modern Origins and Its Role after Devolution*.

[78] The vision was that of many but particularly Winston Roddick CMG, KC, the First Counsel General, Sir Christopher Pitchford, then leader of the Wales and Chester Circuit, solicitors, Huw Williams and Michael Jones, supported by Professor Thomas Watkin KC, Professor David Miers, David Lambert and Marie Navarro of Cardiff University as reflected in the Welsh Legal History Society, founded in 1999. The success of Legal Wales has been reflected in annual conferences each October since 2003.

has achieved the structure of government that enables it to make the laws a nation should have and the ability to enact those distinctive laws. That basic question is best addressed by asking in turn five difficult questions.

1.3.1 *Does the Nature of the Powers of the Executive and Legislative Branches of Government Provided to Wales Measure up to What a Nation Needs?*

Answer: No.

The Government of Wales Act 2006 (in what is described as phase 2 of Welsh devolution) effected a fundamental change. It paved the way for the conferral of real legislative powers that took place after the 2011 referendum. There was, however, no re-examination or principles-based analysis of the question whether the subject matter of the range of powers inherited from the Secretary of State as a member of the executive branch of government was the right starting point for conferring full and real legislative powers. The provisions of the Bill dealing with the subjects in which the Senedd was to be given competence (and the exceptions within those subject areas) were drafted at a late stage and in anticipation of further revision before they took effect. As one of the drafters commented on the draft schedule,[79] in which the subjects were set out:

[79] Schedule 7 to the Bill that became the Government of Wales Act 2006, as appears from documents disclosed in relation to the *Agricultural Sector (Wales) Bill.*

> Unusually, however, the main function of Part I [of Schedule 7] at the time when the legislation is being considered by Parliament is political rather than legal. It is extremely unlikely that, by the time of the referendum, whatever we say here will be accurate. If the provisions require to be amended and finessed by Order in Council at that time, there seems little point in dotting every 'I' and crossing every 't' at this stage . . .. What the provisions need to do at this point is to describe in pretty general (though hopefully largely accurate) terms the subjects that would be devolved if Bill-making competence were to be conferred on the Assembly and Royal Assent and to point up exceptions which are substantial or potentially politically controversial. So I think that brevity is very desirable.

Nor was there any public debate or any public scrutiny as to whether the limited powers were in any way justifiable for a nation. The public were simply asked to vote on the question of whether the legislature should be able to make laws on the matters for which it already had powers. Nor, once it was accepted that there be legislative devolution, was the question answered as to why there remained any basis for the different treatment of Wales to Scotland.

In short, the creation of a legislative branch of government was a fundamental change. Its impact was not subject to a principles-based analysis and was not publicly scrutinised in relation to the scope of the powers that a nation's legislature should be able to exercise,[80] even when there was a further change to the constitutional position in

[80] As the Supreme Court pointed out at paragraph 42 of the *Agricultural Sector (Wales) Bill*:

phase 4.[81] It appears that this was due to the need to achieve political compromise.[82]

It is therefore safe to conclude that the legislative powers of the Senedd rest on a basis that is historic and which was no longer relevant after 2011 when Wales moved away from Executive Devolution. The powers provided for in the 2006 Act should have been based on a rational, logical, coherent and stable scheme – a scheme that a nation should have, if it is to be in a position to make and delineate its own laws in line with the principles set out earlier and the principle in relation to the Union to be considered later.

1.3.2 Is There Undue Complexity?

Answer: Yes.

A summary of the areas of law in which the Senedd will generally make law[83] shows at first sight a seemingly wide

> The current legislative competence of the Assembly has to be determined by an interpretation of the terms of Part 4 and Schedule 7 and not by reference to the way in which functions may have been distributed between the UK Parliament and UK Ministers on the one hand and the Assembly on the other in the first and second phases of Welsh devolution.

[81] See *Delivering a Reserved Powers Model of Devolution for Wales*, September 2015, a report published by the Wales Governance Centre and the Constitution Unit.

[82] See Dylan Hughes (2023) '*Harri a Harold: Effaith hanes Cymru ar gyfraith Cymru (Henry and Harold: The Impact of Welsh History on Welsh Law)* (Barn: Mawrth).

[83] The Future of Welsh Law Consultation, www.gov.wales/sites/default/files/consultations/2020-01/the-future-of-welsh-law-consultation-document.pdf – annex A and B.

scope of the matters in which it can make law, but it can immediately be seen that large areas of law are missing:

1. Agriculture, animals and plants
2. Food
3. Environment and natural resources
4. Planning, building and land
5. Culture, sport and historic environment
6. Economic development and tourism
7. Education and skills
8. Fire and rescue
9. Health and social care
10. Housing
11. Transport
12. Local government
13. Public administration
14. Senedd and legislation
15. Taxation (limited)
16. Welsh language

However, the legal position is very much more complex than appears from this simple summary. Although the Senedd has a general power to legislate on any matter (as devolution is on a 'reserved powers model'), that legislative power is very substantially constrained by the reservations set out in two schedules.[84] The schedules run to over forty pages compared to the seventeen pages that suffice to restrict the law-making powers of the Scottish Parliament.

[84] Schedules 7A and 7B inserted into the Government of Wales Act 2006.

The detail in the schedules underlines further the unnecessary complexity:

- The first of the schedules comprises 3 parts, one setting out 8 General Reservations, one setting out 179 Specific Reservations and a third part setting out General Provisions, which in effect provide exceptions to the Reservations.
- The second of the schedules comprises 2 parts, one setting out General Restrictions and a second part that provides for exceptions to the General Restrictions. 'General Restrictions' is not entirely an apt title for, although it imposes wide ranging restrictions on the powers of the Senedd to legislate, it does so in a manner that is remarkable for its detail and complexity.

If a subject matter is reserved by the schedules, then the Senedd cannot make law if it 'relates to'[85] that matter, a phrase that adds to the complexity and which may be argued to be wide-ranging in its effect.

The scope of the reservations and the exceptions are so complex that it makes operation and understanding of the Senedd's powers very difficult,[86] even for those who are highly specialised in their knowledge of the

[85] This term is defined in s.108A(6):

> The question whether a provision of an Act of the Assembly relates to a reserved matter is determined by reference to the purpose of its provision, having regard (among other things) to its effect in all the circumstances.

[86] See the chart at page 49 of the McAllister/Williams Commission report.

legislation.[87] As there has been no transfer of general criminal or civil law-making powers or of the judicial branch of government, there are further provisions that give the Senedd power to enforce the laws it passes, but again drafted in uncertain and complex terms.

There can be no doubt that this complexity also produces a severe democratic and accountability deficit, as the division of responsibility between Wales and the Union is so defectively structured. To add to the democratic and accountability deficit and to enhance the complexity, the schedule is subject to change by that UK Parliament. A glance at the schedules will show the revision that takes place as the law made by the UK Parliament changes.

This complexity and the nature of the reservations and the restrictions are not compatible with the principles I have set out.

1.3.3 *What Is the Significance of the Absence of the Judicial Branch of Government and the Lack of a Separate or Distinct Jurisdiction?*

Answer: Considerable. Wales' position in respect of the judiciary and the jurisdiction is unique.

[87] The general complexity is evident from the detailed discussion in Watkin with Greenberg at pages 86–94, 100–102 and at pages 59–62 of *Justice in Wales for the People of Wales*.

1.3.3.1 The Judiciary

It is first right to emphasise that various significant steps have been taken by the judiciary of England and Wales to signify the separate identity of Wales within the judicial system of England and Wales. The steps include:

- The giving of directions for the hearing of administrative law cases in Wales on 30 June 1999 (following on from a commitment made at the first conference of UK judges convened by Lord Irvine in London on 9 April 1999)[88] and the subsequent creation of an Administrative Court for Wales in August 2000.
- The Court of Appeal has sat regularly in Cardiff from October 1999.
- The Supreme Court sat in Cardiff in July 2019.
- A Mercantile Court for Wales was established and opened by Lord Bingham in May 2000.
- The Lord Chancellor's Standing Committee on the Welsh Language was established in 1999 to strengthen the use of Welsh in the Courts.[89]
- The Association of the Judges of Wales was founded on 11 October 2008[90] and a Committee for Wales of the Judges' Council was set up in 2011.

[88] The first hearings were in the week of 15 February 2000.

[89] An Advisory Committee on Criminal Justice to the National Assembly was established in July 2001 but lapsed with changes to criminal justice arrangements made in London.

[90] With Sir Malcolm Pill as its President, Sir Roderick Evans as its Secretary and Judge Milwyn Jarman KC as Treasurer.

- The judiciary was also instrumental in arranging seminars with the Richard Commission on 7 February 2003, the All Wales Convention (chaired by Sir Emyr Jones Parry) in April 2009 and the Commission on Devolution in Wales (chaired by Sir Paul Silk) 17 May 2013.
- The judiciary has strongly supported the Legal Wales annual conferences begun in 2003 at the initiative of Legal Wales.

However, in addition to the deficiencies in the powers of the executive and legislative branches of government, there is a total absence of the Welsh nation's own judicial branch of government, beyond the tiny transfer in 1998 referred to earlier[91] and a small increment in 2017 through the creation of the office of President of Welsh Tribunals and associated provisions.[92]

Wales is unique in the world in not having its own judicial branch of government, for unlike any other nation with a legislature, Wales has not been put in a position to interpret or develop its own laws through its own judiciary. That would ordinarily be achieved for a nation, as it is in Scotland, by judges who live in the nation and understand the way in which the law enacted by its legislature is to be interpreted and developed in the context of its polity and

[91] In 2007, the UK Parliament enacted legislation that terminated departmental sponsorship of tribunals and created a separate judicial structure for tribunals in consequence of the Leggatt Report of 2001. The Welsh government proposed in June 2023 to establish an independent structure, www.gov.wales/new-tribunal-system-wales-white-paper-html. No legislation had been brought forward.

[92] Ss.59–64 of the Wales Act 2017.

nationhood. Moreover, there is the important constitutional expectation of interdependency between the executive, legislative and judicial branches of government. In practice it has been my experience that good governance and good law-making requires a close working relationship between the leadership of the judiciary and the executive and legislature.

Moreover, although many of the laws made by the Senedd are drafted and debated by those whose language is Welsh as well as English,[93] and despite this being implicit in the legislative provisions for equal status of both languages for 'all purposes',[94] there is no express right to have the laws considered by judges who understand Welsh as one of their own languages.[95] This is in striking contrast to Canada where it is considered a fundamental right to have a judge on the court who understands the language and does not have to rely

[93] See Dylan Hughes (2023) *Cyfraith Cymru, cyfreithwyr a hynt y Gymraeg wrth lywodraethu Cymru (Welsh Law, Welsh Lawyers and the Standing of the Welsh Language in the Governance of Wales)* (Barn, Ebrill).

[94] See s.5 of the Legislation (Wales) Act/Deddf Deddfwriaeth (Cymru) 2019. Similar provisions were made in the Government of Wales Acts of 1998 and 2006.

[95] See *R (Driver) v Rhondda Cynon Taff Borough Council* [2020] EWCA Civ 1759 as to the approach the Court of Appeal has decided should be taken to the interpretation of bilingual legislation. An excellent review of this decision was contained in a paper by Dylan Hughes delivered to the Commonwealth Magistrates and Judges Association at Cardiff on 12 September 2023: *Bilingual Law in Wales (and England): The Implications of Law Being Made in Two Languages* (2024) 45 Statute Law Review, Issue No 1. See also Dr Catrin Flûr Huws *Bilingual Statutory Interpretation and the United Kingdom: Domestic Law and International Experiences* (2024) 45 Statute Law Review, Issue No 1.

on translation or expert evidence.[96] My experience of sitting in Qatar reinforces the absolute necessity of this.

There have been many calls for Wales to have its own judicial branch of government,[97] but despite the steps taken, this fundamental issue remains unaddressed.

1.3.3.2 Jurisdiction

In addition, Wales does not have its own legal jurisdiction.[98] It is included within the jurisdiction of 'England and Wales' and in a way that is inevitably subordinate. The single jurisdiction for England and Wales continues because a Welsh jurisdiction was not created on the transfer of legislative power to the Senedd. This created a unique situation as, Wales apart, each legislature has its own jurisdiction, not least because one of the purposes of a jurisdiction is to demarcate difference in law.[99] In a real sense, the effect is that there is no 'Welsh law' as such: the laws passed by the Senedd 'extend' to the jurisdiction of England and Wales and therefore are part

96 *R v Beaulac* [1999] 1 SCR 768.

97 See Lord Carlile of Berriew KC (June 2000) *The Evolution of Devolution*, David Lloyd George Memorial Lecture; Sir Roderick Evans (19 February 2010) *Devolution and the Administration of Justice*, The Lord Callaghan Memorial Lecture Swansea University; Sir Malcolm Pill (9 October 2009) lecture to the Legal Wales Conference.

98 The specific problems relating to criminal justice are not covered in this lecture. They are set out in detail in the Report of the Commission on Justice in Wales. The issues are further discussed in R. Jones and R. Wyn Jones (2022) *The Welsh Criminal Justice System – On the Jagged edge*, University of Wales Press.

99 England and Wales is the only legal jurisdiction in the world in which two legislatures make different laws about the same subject matter.

of the 'law of England and Wales'.[100] Similarly, all laws passed by the UK Parliament in respect of England 'extend' to England and Wales. This means that laws are English law or Welsh law in a separate sense only if specifically made 'applicable' to England or Wales respectively.

In what might be termed 'a neat legislative provision', the Wales Act 2017 has recognised that there is 'Welsh law' by its reference to 'the law that applies in Wales includes a body of Welsh law made by the Assembly and Welsh Ministers'.[101] However, the explanatory notes underline the fact that this is in reality little more than a gesture[102] and changed nothing. This issue should have been addressed like the question of the

[100] It is not entirely clear when this phrase was first adopted. As referred to above, s.3 of the Wales and Berwick on Tweed Act 1746 made it unnecessary to refer to Wales in legislation because it was included when a reference was made to England. However, with the repeal of that Act in 1967, it was necessary to expressly refer to Wales to signify when laws extend to England and Wales (and not for the UK as a whole, Great Britain, Scotland or Northern Ireland).

[101] Wales Act 2017 s.1 provides:

> Recognition of Welsh law
>
> (1) The law that applies in Wales includes a body of Welsh law made by the Assembly and the Welsh Ministers.
> (2) The purpose of this section is, with due regard to the other provisions of this Act, to recognise the ability of the Assembly and the Welsh Ministers to make law forming part of the law of England and Wales.

[102] The Notes read: 'The purpose of making this declaratory statement does not in any way affect the devolution boundary and in particular the fact that the single legal jurisdiction is a reserved matter.'

creation of a judicial branch of government, when the legislative powers were transferred, but it was not.

Much has been said about the supposed practical difficulties of establishing a separate jurisdiction.[103] There are none as is shown by the fact that both Scotland and Northern Ireland have separate jurisdictions within the UK.

1.3.4 *What Has Been the Effect of Brexit?*

Answer: Considerable, as there has been a failure to provide a proper governance structure to replace what was provided when the UK was a member of the EU.

As mentioned, the context for the original grant to and exercise of many executive and legislative powers in Wales was the UK's membership of the EU. That membership had a profound effect on the nature and extent of transfers, the way many of the powers were exercised by the Welsh government within the framework of detailed EU legislation in relation to the functioning of the EU internal market and on the way the Union functioned, given the role of the EU Commission in so many matters. As was observed in 2017 by the House of Lords European Committee:[104]

[103] See, for example, the speech of Jack Straw when Lord Chancellor on 3 December 2009 cited in Timothy H. Jones *Wales, Devolution and Sovereignty* 33 (2012) Statute Law Review 151 at page 160.

[104] July 2107 Report *Brexit Devolution* (4th report Session 2017–19, HL Paper 9) at page 3: See also the Report of the House of Lords Constitution Committee 11 May 2016 (HL Paper 149).

> EU law is interwoven with the devolution settlements, and throughout this period, the supremacy of that EU law, and its interpretation by the Court of Justice of the EU, have helped to hold the UK together and maintain the integrity of its internal market.

The Committee concluded:

> The European Union has been, in effect, part of the glue holding the United Kingdom together since 1997.

Although assurances were given that leaving the EU would make no change to the powers that had been conferred on the Welsh legislature and executive, there was no proper examination of the adjustments that were necessary to the Union that is the UK. It should have been clear that mechanisms had to be created to replace the role of the EU, particularly in relation to the common standards and other rules. These were required for a common approach to the UK internal market (the market between England, Northern Ireland, Scotland and Wales) when that market took the place of the EU internal market, which encompassed the then twenty-eight Member States including the UK.

It was envisaged that in place of the detailed legal framework established by the EU through its institutions, the policy, rules and standards for the UK internal market would be set by a system of Common Frameworks[105] – agreements

[105] See the First Report of the House of Lords Common Frameworks Scrutiny Committee: *Common Frameworks: Building a Cooperative Union* (HL Paper 259).

between the four governments of varying lengths and complexity covering many aspects of the internal market. Progress on putting these in place was delayed by the pandemic and then considerably undermined by the unilateral decision of the UK government to proceed with what became the UK Internal Market Act 2020. The UK government published in July 2020 a White Paper[106] outlining its intention to create a legislative underpinning for the UK internal market, replacing what had previously been provided by EU law, on the basis that Common Frameworks could not on their own guarantee the integrity of the UK internal market. There was no consultation with the Welsh or Scottish governments about this change in approach; nor was there any before the UK Internal Market Bill was published in September 2020[107].

Common Frameworks apart, there is no other effective mechanism in place for the cooperative exercise of powers on a joint basis for the UK internal market. The Joint Ministerial Committee[108] proved ineffective after Brexit and

[106] CP278.

[107] The McAllister/Williams Commission reached a similar conclusion about the status of intergovernmental relations in chapter 4 of its Final Report. It recommended at pages 58 and 123 that there be legislation 'for inter-governmental mechanisms so as to secure a duty of co-operation and parity of esteem between the governments of the UK'.

[108] A Memorandum of Agreement was first made between the governments in 1999 and successively revised. The second report of the Silk Commission chapter 5 sets out a summary of the way intergovernmental relations were working at the date the report was published in March 2014.

the successor arrangements established in 2022[109] with the Prime Minister and Devolved Heads of Government Council at its apex and the Inter-ministerial Standing Committees, Inter-ministerial Groups and different levels of mechanism for dispute resolution beneath have yet to show there has been a material change.[110] Other necessary adjustments consequent on Brexit have not been made.

1.3.5 Should There Be Concern about the Operation and Nature of the Union?

Answer: Yes

One of the strengths of the way constitutions have operated historically, particularly the UK constitution, is that those involved in governance have abided by understandings of the way constitutions should operate through constitutional conventions. A central part of the constitutional arrangements for the Union made in 1997–1998 was the

[109] Following Lord Dunlop's Review of UK Government Capability (report dated November 2019 but only published on 24 March 2021). The inaugural meeting took place in Blackpool on 10 November 2022 attended by the Prime Minister, the First Ministers of Scotland and Wales and other ministers, https://assets.publishing.service.gov.uk/media/605b7749d3bf7f2f132f5b4a/Lord_Dunlop_s_review_into_UK_Government_Union_Capability.pdf.

[110] In 2021 and 2022, a quarterly report, *Intergovernmental Relations Quarterly Report*, was published first by the Cabinet Office and then by the then Department of Levelling Up, Housing and Communities as its Secretary of State was the UK Minister for Intergovernmental Arrangements until July 2024. An annual report for 2023 was published in 2024.

development of a constitutional convention – the Sewel Convention[111] – which provided that the UK Parliament would not normally legislate in matters within the competence of the Northern Ireland, Scottish and Welsh legislatures without the consent of those legislatures. The convention worked reasonably well until the legislation consequent on Brexit. Since Brexit consent has been refused on far too many occasions; changes have been imposed rather than agreed. The process began with the EU (Withdrawal Agreement) Act 2020 and the UK Internal Market Act and continued until the General Election of July 2024.[112] Undermining this convention has serious long-term implications.[113]

The breakdown of the Sewel Convention has been exacerbated by the emergence of a lack of political consensus on the nature of the Union. In 2014 Carwyn Jones as First Minister, explained Wales' perspective of the Union at the Institute of Government;[114] the position

[111] Subsequently recognised in legislation (s.2 of the Wales Act 2017) but determined by the UK Supreme Court to operate on a political not legal basis and so unenforceable in the courts: *R (Miller) v The Secretary of State for Exiting the European Union* [2017] UKSC 5 at paragraphs 140–151.

[112] For more detail, see Professor Richard Rawlings *Wales and the United Kingdom: a territorial constitutional policy drive*, in Territory, Politics, Governance (2022) 10, 714–732 at 725–728.

[113] See chapter 4 of the Report of the House of Lords Committee on the Constitution (January 2022): *Respect and Co-operation: Building a Stronger Union for 21 Century*, HL Paper 142; chapter 4 of the Report of the McAllister/Willimas Commission at 44–46 and 52.

[114] 15 October 2014, Our Future Union: A perspective from Wales, www.instituteforgovernment.org.uk/event/keynote-speech-rt-hon-carwyn-jones-am-minister-wales-our-future-union.

was set out more formally by the Welsh Government in 2021:[115]

> Whatever its historical origins, the United Kingdom is best seen now as a voluntary association of nations taking the form of a multi-national state, whose members share and redistribute resources and risks amongst themselves to advance their common interests. Wales is committed to this association, which must be based on the recognition of popular sovereignty in each part of the UK; Parliamentary sovereignty as traditionally understood no longer provides a sound foundation for this evolving constitution.

1.4 What Principles Should Apply to the Law-making Position of a Nation within a Union?

Having outlined the history of Welsh law and the restoration of law-making powers, and having provided an assessment based on the answers to five difficult questions, I can complete the consideration of the six principles that should govern the choice of laws for a nation on a principled and pragmatic basis.[116] I do so by addressing the sixth principle – the principle applicable to a nation within a Union.

115 *Reforming our Union: Shared Governance in the UK, Second Edition June 2021*, www.gov.wales/sites/default/files/publications/2021-06/reforming-our-union-shared-governance-in-the-uk-june-2021-0.pdf. The legal position is clear – it is a Union under the Crown in Parliament and is legally binding on all the parts of the Union unless and until Parliament changes the position by Act of Parliament.

116 I set these out at pages <7> and following earlier in this chapter.

As I have already set out, the system of government for Wales has emerged from compromise and incremental change based on what had gone before. Little emphasis has been put on points of principle. It is time to think again and consider what powers a nation needs and how that should be determined in circumstances in which the nation is part of a Union.

It should be obvious that consideration must be given to the nature and purpose of the Union when considering the law-making powers needed for nations within a Union, as the nature and purpose of the Union are essential in delineating the distribution of law-making power within the Union. This point must be particularly stressed in relation to the UK, as although many speak of strengthening the Union which is the UK, insufficient thought is given to the nature and purpose of such a Union. As has been remarked 'A policy of drift will never result in united strength'.[117]

1.4.1 *What Is Needed for a Nation within a Union*

In explaining this sixth principle as to the laws appropriate for a nation within a Union, what is central is the nature and purpose of the Union and certainty as to the complex questions that arise as to the distribution and exercise of powers of the three branches of government across a Union of nations.

As mentioned already, although various approaches are possible within a Union, there are two main approaches.

[117] Quoted in Colley at page 156.

One is the top-down approach where consideration is given to the fields of law and policy where powers are to be granted to the nation to facilitate the adoption of laws and policies best suited to the needs or wishes of the nations of the Union, which provide for better accountability and participation in government and which lighten the load of the central government.[118] The other, a bottom-up approach, is that the nations or states comprising the Union should determine those areas of law that they should pool but retain for the nations what the nations consider it is best for them to retain.

While it may not be necessary to choose one or the other of these approaches, the purpose of the Union is the central determinant of the scope and exercise of power respectively by the Union government and the governments of the constituent nations or states. For example, where a Union has as its purpose a single internal market or a wide economic union, then very difficult questions arise, as experience has shown, as to the extent of issues that are said to involve economic matters, as so much can be argued to involve an economic matter. In other areas where the purpose of the Union either includes or excludes a specific purpose, then the difficulties can be few. For example, defence and the maintenance of armed forces were never powers allocated to the EU; and it has not been argued that defence and foreign affairs are other than matters for the Union government in the UK and not for its constituent nations. These are defined subject areas and not areas that give rise to argument.

[118] This was essentially the approach of Kilbrandon – see chapter 16, particularly paragraph 699.

After determining the purpose of the Union and the needs of the nation based on the five principles I have set out, then there are a number of further factors:

- First, there will be some powers that need to be exercised in co-operation under a stable legal, political and administrative framework and mechanism. A good example is the KBF (the Industrial development Bank) in Germany where the Lande (the states that comprise the Federal Republic of Germany) have an institutional membership. This contrasts with the creation of the UK Infrastructure Bank (a British replacement for the European Investment Bank) where no stake or direct interest was given to Northern Ireland, Scotland or Wales. The Treasury can, under the Infrastructure Bank Act 2023, even make regulations in relation to matters within the powers of the national legislatures after consultation with the national legislatures.[119]
- Second, there must be coherence.
- Third, the result must be practical and a division of powers that is too complex avoided, as there is a need for ease of understanding and accountability.
- Fourth, the comparative size and economic power of the entities that comprise the Union will be relevant.
- Fifth, in the Union that is the UK, there is the complicating factor that England is by far the biggest and wealthiest nation and that the Union government is also the government of England, often making it difficult to determine in which capacity it is acting.

[119] Section 2 (8).

- Sixth, there must also be a fair and equal dispute resolution mechanism.

1.4.2 *The Question of Sovereignty and Federalisation*

In resolving these questions, it is not in my view helpful to conduct the debate through the lens of 'sovereignty'. Some regard the traditional nineteenth-century view of sovereignty best expressed by Dicey as central to the issues.[120] Others starting with Carwyn Jones when First Minister of Wales and then more formally the Welsh Government, as just mentioned, have put forward a different view of sovereignty to that of Dicey. Some discussion is necessary, if for no other reason than to dispel myths and deal with practical issues.[121] This can be illustrated by the provisions of Schedule 3 to the Subsidy Control Act 2022, which enables legislation of the Senedd in respect of subsidies in Wales to be challenged in the High Court of England and Wales (rather than the Supreme

[120] There has always been an argument that the sovereignty of Parliament is incompatible with achieving an embedded settlement of the distribution of executive, legislative and judicial powers between the nations that comprise the UK – a process that can be described as federalism – see, for example, *Dicey's Law of the Constitution* (1885), Oxford University Press.

[121] The decision of the majority of the Supreme Court in *Recovery of Medical Costs for Asbestosis Diseases (Wales) Bill* further complicates the position. The view of the majority was that, although it was not entitled to review any proceedings or judgement of the UK Parliament in relation to legislation it passed, it was able to review the judgement of the Senedd even where it had the full powers of the UK Parliament.

Court, which has sole jurisdiction over its legislative competence), even though no such challenge can be made to legislation made for England by the UK Parliament. The reason given for the inability to challenge legislation of the UK Parliament was the sovereignty of Parliament and the first Article of the Bill of Rights 1688, which prohibits the courts questioning proceedings in Parliament – that is to say, the UK Parliament, not the National Parliaments.

Although some discussion of sovereignty is necessary, if the debates focus on sovereignty, there is a real danger for four principal reasons:

- Although in pure legal theory a nation-state that is not part of a Union is traditionally treated as 'sovereign' or called a 'sovereign state', as it has an unconstrained ability to make any law it wants, there are in fact real practical constraints arising from multilateral treaties it enters into or bilateral treaties made with specific states.
- The use of the term 'sovereignty' has given rise to a confusion between what has been termed a pragmatic definition of sovereignty and an ideological one, as pointed out by Dr Rowan Williams in May 2023.[122]
- Sovereignty has become a populist term, as was evident in the arguments over Brexit and particularly in relation to the special arrangements for Northern Ireland.

[122] In his address to the Commonwealth Association of Legislative Counsel's Europe Conference on 24 May 2023: *Law and Sovereignty: Questions of Definition, Published in the Loophole*, The Journal of the Association, Issue 2, September 2023 at page 51.

- The issues are better addressed by concentrating on the pragmatic. For example, the Trade and Cooperation Agreement between the UK and the EU made in 2021 places considerable limits on the power of the UK Parliament to legislate in areas such as state subsidies as is evident from the terms of the Subsidy Control Act 2022. However, that Agreement was made on a pragmatic basis and no issue was raised as to its effect on sovereignty.

Nor is it necessary to expend energy on terms such as 'Federal', 'Semi-Federal' or 'Quasi Federal'.[123] These again have emotive connotation as they raise the argument as to the need for a written constitution and over sovereignty. In the debates on 'home rule all round' in 1920, federalism was seen as being fundamental to the issues, but one so problematic in resolution that it was better not to address it and for the UK simply to muddle along as had been done for ten centuries.[124] I have therefore not entered into the issue of federalisation. although it has been discussed by the McAllister/Williams Commission.[125] The issues can be addressed pragmatically without reference to the federal question.

[123] See Sir David G. T. Williams QC 1974 lecture at pages 85–89 for the argument that federalism might be preferable to an unentrenched scheme of legislative devolution, as such a scheme was federalism without the courage of its convictions. See Sir David Willam Lord Morris lecture 1993 and Sir David Williams Inaugural Lecture 2000.

[124] There is a good account in Coupland at pages 315–335.

[125] Final Report at pages 80–84, 95–112 and 124.

1.5 What Role Should the Principles Play?

Having explained the position of a nation within a Union, it is now possible to draw some general conclusions about the law a nation needs.

1.5.1 *The Practicalities*

Wales was, as explained, allocated some powers of executive government, including the power to make regulations, at a time when there was no realistic alternative but to take what was on offer. Since then, as is more usually the position in similar circumstances, argument has been centred on relative strength and political wrangling between those interested in acquiring or retaining powers.

Accidents of history, relative political strength and political wrangling will often determine the powers of government given to a nation to make laws. However, if a nation or the Union of nations is to achieve the stability necessary to benefit the nation and the Union, then the question as to the laws a nation needs and the powers to make them must be addressed with rationality, logic and coherence based on the principles I have set out. It should not be based on political wrangling between those interested in acquiring or retaining powers.

1.5.2 *The Value of Principles in Enabling the Peoples of a Nation to Secure Their Ambitions and Their Identity*

The first of the questions I posed in this chapter was why a nation needed its own laws. The five principles identified in answer to that question were (1) the promotion of the nation's ambitions and values, (2) the promotion and strengthening of its distinct language and culture, (3) its capacity to make and develop the law, (4) its ability to create and administer simpler and more accessible laws and (5) its ability to address the concerns of the people of the nation. These are the principles that should primarily govern the question as to laws needed for a nation. Where a nation is part of a Union, the purpose of the Union is a sixth principle as it is determinative of the powers that the Union needs and powers that should be shared with the nations of the Union. These are certainly the principles that determine the distinct laws Wales, as a nation, should be able to make, with the branches of government and powers necessary to enact and develop them.

1.6 What Are the Options for Law-making Powers for the Welsh Nation Based on the Principles?

It is now possible to test the principles through using Wales as a case study by asking the question as to how Wales as a nation can achieve a rational, logical, coherent and stable system of law governed by the principles I have enumerated? This question is best answered through the examination of the realistic options for the law-making powers Wales as a nation should have in the context of the Union, as the extent of the powers depends on what is required to meets the needs of Wales as a nation within a Union.

1.6.1 *Option 1: The Existing System*

The opportunity to restore to Wales as a nation its own laws was achieved through the acceptance of the very limited offer made by the UK government in 1997 to the transfer of the powers of the executive branch of government (with its subordinate law-making powers) from the Secretary of State to the National Assembly. When powers of the legislative branch of government were transferred in 2011, there was no offer to reconsider the scope of what laws could be made in Wales for Wales once it had a legislature. In the further change in 2017 to the reserved powers model, there was no justification for the extensive reservations, despite the then Welsh government's strenuous efforts exemplified by the publication of its own Government and Laws in Wales Bill.[126] Nor on either occasion in 2011 or 2017 was the different treatment of the Scottish and Welsh nations justified.

I do not think it possible to dispute the fact that the way in which the current powers have been defined does not permit laws to be made in a rational, logical, coherent and stable way. Two examples must suffice:

- It does not permit laws to be made to deal with basic interlocking problems. For example, as the Report of the Commission on Justice in Wales demonstrates, the government of Wales has no power to develop more effective and coherent laws and policies for dealing with crime relating to or fuelled by drugs, or addressing youth crime, or dealing

[126] *Government and Laws in Wales Bill*, www.gov.wales/sites/default/files/publications/2018-09/wales-bill-draft_0.pdf.

with prisoners on release or determining how there is a coordination of law and long-term policy on issues in health, education and criminal justice, which are plainly interrelated. The people of England, Scotland and Northern Ireland have the benefits of such coordination. The Welsh nation is denied it for no conceivable justification.

- Although health, education, ambulance and fire services in Wales are entirely within the responsibility of the Senedd, the Strikes (Minimum Service Level) Act 2023 enabled the UK government to set minimum service levels in Wales for these services, even though it has no responsibility for these services and therefore lacks much of the necessary knowledge to set minimum standards. It asserted it had the right to do this as it 'related to' the power of the UK government in respect of employment rights and industrial relations.[127] Although this was disputed by the Senedd, the fact that the Senedd was right did not matter, as the UK government was able to make that the law for Wales through the use of its majority in the UK Parliament. It was notable that when standards were set for ambulance services in December 2023,[128] these were not applied to Wales. The Employment Rights Bill 2025 repeals the Act.

Maintaining the existing system is an option. However, taking together the absence of Wales' own judicial branch of government, the deficiencies in the powers of the Senedd and

[127] Schedule 7A part 2, paragraph 141.

[128] The Strikes (Minimum Service Levels: NHS Ambulances and NHS Patient Transport Service) Regulations 2023.

their interrelationship to the Union powers and the way in which the UK government exercises the powers of the Union, it follows from the principles I have set out that the current system as a system does not meet those principles. In short, Wales is denied what a nation should have.

1.6.2 *Option 2: Transfer of the Powers of the Judicial Branch of Government and Widening Specific Legislative Power*

A second option is to transfer the powers of the judicial branch of government, to add more powers of the legislative branch of government and to create a simpler structure, so that the principal deficiencies are cured.

It follows from the principles I have set out that a much wider range of laws is needed. The restrictions on the law-making powers need to be narrowed. If that were the option pursued then I would anticipate that the following would be examples of the laws the Senedd could enact.

- *Criminal law and policing*:[129] The reasons for transferring responsibility for criminal justice are set out at length in the report of the Commission, *Justice in Wales for the People of Wales*. The report is premised purely on the practical and pragmatic, not the wider issues canvassed in this chapter. There has been no reasoned answer to it. One illustration of why the present position is untenable is demonstrated by the fact that Wales cannot make its own dangerous dogs

[129] See schedule 7 paragraphs 39 and following.

legislation, although Wales has a very different economy, demography, geography and traditions to England.

- *Family law*: The Commission also set out the reasons why family justice should be transferred. However, its remit was not interpreted as extending to broader aspects of family law. There are, however, cogent reasons why family law should be law a nation can make, as the nature of the family is so fundamental to society.[130] In many societies, the law relating to the family was regarded as personal to the family and many states have recognised different systems as operating concurrently. Family law today extends to the recognition of partnerships and the rights that arise on dissolution. Here is a real need to reform financial provisions on divorce and the ending of other relationships.[131]
- *Succession and inheritance*: Again, these laws are integral to a nation as quite apart from taxation, the methods by which assets can be held or transferred or the restrictions that can be imposed are an important part of the way in which transmitted wealth can be protected or the inequalities arising from it minimised.
- *Civil and private law*: Numerous examples can be taken from civil or private law – remedies and privacy. Although some aspects of privacy are the subject of human rights

[130] Lord Morris of Aberavon explained in his 2001 Lord Merlyn Rees lecture why the issue of the family in Wales was one of the three most important issues faced by the National Assembly as the nuclear family was no longer a characteristic of Welsh Life with the rise of the one parent family.

[131] See Osian Rees, *Devolution and Family Law in Wales: A Potential for Doing Things Differently* (2012) 33 Statute Law Review 192–206.

protection, there is a margin within which a nation should be able to determine the extent of the privacy to which people are entitled.

Making these changes would not be difficult and would have the benefit of simplifying the complexity of the current system. Nor should it be difficult to transfer the judicial branch of government and create a Welsh jurisdiction as recommended by the Commission on Justice in Wales. No reason for denying the Welsh nation its own missing branch of government has been given. It is always possible that it is believed that Wales is not capable of exercising judicial power; but this is irrational as it ignores the contribution Welsh judges have made and their originality. It is not just a contribution to English law[132] but to the law of the United States[133] (Thomas Jefferson, John Marshall and Charles Evans Hughes) and Australia (Sir Samuel Griffith). As no explanation has been given, it is possible that it is thought that giving Wales the powers of the judicial branch of government might make it too much like Scotland and therefore have to be treated in the same way. As no explanation has been given, it is probable that there is no rational explanation but impossible to provide an answer without the explanation for the denial.

[132] It is often argued that Welsh Judges made a significant contribution to English law. See Seaborne Davies (1967) *Welsh Makers of English Law*, BBC broadcast published in (2003) 3 Welsh Legal History Society 1.

[133] See Sir David Williams QC Lord Morris Lecture 1993 and Sir David G. T. Willaims QC *The Law of England and Wales: The Welsh Contribution* (2005), vol. 12 Transactions of the Cymmrodorion 161.

However, I do not consider that this option meets the principles I have set out. Although the transfer of the judicial branch of government and the provision of a separate jurisdiction is essential for the reasons I have explained, there are two principal deficiencies. First, the powers of the Senedd and the executive would not rest on a basis that is rational, logical, coherent and stable; it is still too complex and premised on a piecemeal rather than a principled and strategic approach. Second, it would not address the fundamental issues relating to the Union or of the machinery necessary for a workable interrelationship of the branches of government within the Union.

1.6.3 Option 3: The General Ability to Make Law Save Where Specified Powers Are Reserved for the Purposes of the Union

The easiest and simplest option is one that meets the principles I have set out and one that is likely to produce a stable system. That is achieved in the most straightforward way by starting from the premise that all powers are allocated to a nation save those that are needed for the purposes of the Union government. Testing the allocation against the other criteria I have set out, the bottom-up approach appears to be preferable, but it is also possible to take the top-down approach. What is essential is that the powers that vest in the Union are the powers needed for the purpose of the Union.

This is again not the place for a detailed consideration of the functions that are required for a Union. One of the schedules to the Government of Wales Act sets out some of the core functions of the Union such as defence and foreign affairs, but its complex and detailed structure is not the best starting point. A better one is the Act of Union Bill[134] introduced into the House of Lords by Lord Lisvane in October 2018. It has twenty-six paragraphs over four pages, which set out the functions of the Union. It is well drafted, concise and provides an excellent starting point for a scheme of central functions that is logical and shows that there are clear matters for the Union such as the currency, monetary policy, defence and foreign affairs.

Resolving the Union function is but part of the need. It is clear from experience that although functions such as defence and foreign policy can be clearly defined areas for a Union, there are difficult areas such as those relating to the economy which are a function of the Union and a function of the nations. It is hard to see how this can be managed without a stable legal structure of which the Union and the national governments are part. This is exemplified by issues that have arisen such as (a) provisions and machinery to ensure coordination of Welsh Government Funding and UK Government Funding from the shared prosperity fund or its successor funds or (b) the need for adequate powers not only for the UK government but also for the national governments in relation to the control of subsidies[135] or (c) the future of the steel industry in Wales.

[134] *Act of Union Bill*, https://publications.parliament.uk/pa/bills/lbill/2017-2019/0132/18132.pdf – schedule of central policy areas.

[135] The powers given in the Subsidy Control Act 2022 to the UK government were not given to the national governments.

We have reached the stage where in my view it is clear that the law relating to the purpose and functions of the Union needs to be reconsidered before there can be the necessary clarity and stability in relation to the scope of the laws the nations should make.

These are difficult problems as was illustrated by the Mission Statements provided for in Part 1 of the Levelling Up and Regeneration Act 2023. Mission statements are intended to provide targets in a range of subjects from education and health to happiness. There is force in the argument that these need to be UK wide to ensure that resources of the UK are distributed so that funds are given to the parts of the Union that need the greatest help in achieving the targets. However, as at the core of the laws a nation makes are laws such as those relating to education and policies consequent upon them, the Union and the nations must set laws and machinery that provide clearly for Union functions and the relationship with national functions. It is a difficult issue, particularly given the dominant position of England.

It is therefore for this primary reason, option 3 is the option that needs the most careful consideration going forward.

Conclusion

At the beginning I asked what laws a nation needs and later asked if Wales is truly a nation? Wales is without doubt a nation, but Wales cannot make the laws that reflects its nationhood and its spirit until it is has the powers to make them and until it has its own judiciary to interpret and develop those laws and as part of the governance of the nation. No stability will be achieved until those issues and the purpose and function of the Union are addressed by consideration of the principles I have set out. The debate must centre on principle, not political wrangling and expediency. This is what is required if the Union that is the UK is to be strengthened and if Wales is to have restored to it proper law-making-powers to which it is entitled as a nation equal to other nations.

2

Laws for Transnational Commerce

English Commercial Law as a System for Transnational Commerce

The Issues

Chapter 1 looked at the laws a nation should be able to make and in that way define its distinctive character and spirit. Wales was used as a case study, as 25 years ago it had law-making powers restored to it, having lost its own law 450 years earlier. Using Wales provided the additional advantage of being able to consider the position of a nation within a Union that is the UK. This chapter and Chapter 3 move to law where the need of a nation is not for law that simply defines its distinctive character and spirit but law that operates transnationally[1] for those engaged in trade between nations – transnational commerce. In doing so, the focus turns from Welsh law[2] to what everyone knows and calls English law and, in particular, to English commercial law[3] as used transnationally and to transnational law.

[1] A subject that Professor Sir Roy Goode introduced into the curriculum of UK Universities in the 1990s.

[2] Not the artificial political construct of what is called the 'law of England and Wales,' which was explained in Chapter 1 at page <46>.

[3] It is apposite to use the term 'commerce' and 'commercial' rather than 'business', the term adopted by the new Business and Property Courts, as the word 'commercial' has such a historic and promotional value to

English commercial law[4] in one sense defines England as a trading nation but it has become, to the UK's advantage, a national system of commercial law used by other nations for transnational commercial transactions. It has been able to meet the needs of transnational commerce, as the national system of law that is most widely used transnationally. However, distinct from a national system used transnationally (such as English commercial law) is transnational law,[5] which has developed since the late nineteenth century

English law, despite the fact that the etymology of commerce is Latin (via France) rather than old or Middle English for 'business'.

4 Commercial law is considered in these two chapters in the sense in which it is most widely used. I do not cover in any detail aspects of public law, including financial stability, the WTO and competition law, or aspects of the law relating to property and security. Consumer law is also outside the scope of these chapters. Cf R. Goode (1998) *Commercial Law in the Next Millenium: The Forty-ninth Hamlyn Lectures*, Sweet & Maxwell (Goode Hamlyn Lectures) at page 8; and Lord Leggatt (November 2021) 4th Jonathan Hirst Memorial Lecture (Lord Leggatt Hirst Memorial Lecture), *What Is the Point of Commercial Law?* [2022] LMCLQ 242 at page 243.

5 Professor Sir Roy Goode in his collection of essays (2018) *The Development of Transnational Commercial Law*, Oxford University Press, proposes the following definition at page vii:

> That set of private law principles and rules, from whatever source, which governs international commercial transactions and is common to legal systems generally or to a significant number of legal systems.

In R. Goode, H. Kronke and E. McKendrick (eds.) (2015) *Transnational Commercial Law: Texts, Cases and Materials*, 2nd edition, Oxford University Press (Goode, K & M) at page 4 there is a discussion of the different uses of the terms.

to address the needs of those engaged in transnational commerce. It is embodied in uniform practices,[6] international standard terms or general principles of law, rules, model laws or international agreements.

The central issue in this chapter and the next is the impact of the profound changes in commerce on law used for transnational commerce and the position of English commercial law. In the twenty-five years since 1997, when Sir Roy Goode gave the last Hamlyn Lectures that specifically considered English commercial law,[7] there have been profound changes to commerce whilst, at the same time, the use of English commercial law for transnational commerce is under challenge.

In this chapter I cover four main issues:

1. What are the key hallmarks of the way English commercial law has met the needs of transnational commerce?
2. Are the profound changes to global commerce that commercial law faces of a different order of magnitude to that seen hitherto?
3. What was it that enabled English commercial law to develop and adapt so successfully to become the dominant national system used in transnational commerce?

[6] There may be international practices or usages that are part of transnational law (see Goode, K & M at pages 36–42); see also *Libyan Arab Foreign Bank v Bankers Trust Co* [1989] Q.B. 728 – whether there was a binding usage to clear dollars through the New York CHIPS system, which would have subjected the transaction to US sanctions during the Iranian assets crisis.

[7] Goode Hamlyn Lectures.

4. How did English commercial law successfully engage with the move towards creating transnational law for some aspects of commerce?

In Chapter 3, after considering the advantages English commercial law retains and the issues it faces, I put forward five options to maintain the position of English commercial law in the light of the profound changes to commerce and the significant effect they are likely to have on the law in the context of the growth of transnational commercial law.

2.1 What Are the Key Hallmarks of the Way English Commercial Law Has Met the Needs of Transnational Commerce?

2.1.1 *The Centrality of Law to Commerce*

In Chapter 1 I explained why law was central to the identity and spirit of a nation. Law is also central to the functioning of market economies and transnational trade and commerce. This is well understood by those engaged in industry, finance and commerce. However, it is not often understood and frequently now forgotten by politicians in some nations when looking at the importance of devoting time, energy and resources to the operation of commercial law. As it appears to operate so well and so seamlessly, it is too often taken for granted by so many. In the UK that is particularly the case.

2.1.2 The Role of English Commercial Law in Providing a National System of Law That Met Needs of Transnational Commerce

It is therefore necessary first to ask why transnational commerce needs law. Cotton LJ,[8] a sound nineteenth-century Chancery judge (and a noted figure skater) was right and remains right in the view he expressed that commerce is based on knowing whom to trust and with whom to deal; few will enter into transnational commercial transactions with those they do not trust. However, law is needed to underpin that trust,[9] to provide for the necessary documentation, to secure finance and to mitigate the risk of insolvency.

[8] *Sanders v Maclean* (1883) 11 QBD 327 – a case on the practice of issuing bills of lading in a set of three originals; see also the opening address by Sir Anthony Lloyd (later Lord Lloyd of Berwick) to the CMI Colloquium on Bills of Lading in Venice (30 May–1 June 1983).

[9] Lord Reed (January 2022) Sultan Azlan Shah Lecture at the Centre for Islamic Studies at Oxford [2022] LMCLQ 232 stated that 'in developed economies, the principal basis of trust is the legal system, citing from his judgment in *R (Unison) v Lord Chancellor* [2107] UKSC 51 at paragraph 71:

> People and businesses need to know, on the one hand, that they will be able to enforce their rights if they have to do so, and, on the other hand, that if they fail to meet their obligations, there is likely to be a remedy against them. It is that knowledge which underpins everyday economic and social relations. That is so, notwithstanding that judicial enforcement of the law is not usually necessary, and notwithstanding that the resolution of disputes by other methods is often desirable.

See also Lord Leggatt Hirst Memorial Lecture at pages 247–250.

Although the phrase 'my word is my bond' epitomises trust, a written contract was usually seen as a back-up containing the necessary detail. Today, commercial law is essential to transnational commerce. It provides the solid framework for transactions, the basis for the documentation needed and specifies rights and duties in the event of the unexpected such as insolvency or force majeure or the failure by a party to carry out the bargain.

As each nation has, for the reasons explained in Chapter 1, its own system of law that reflects the characteristics of the nation, it is necessary to ask what system of law do those engaged in commerce between different nations choose? Simply using a national system that is not understood or accepted by the other party is not a basis that can underpin a transnational commercial transaction. Those engaged in transnational commerce have therefore looked for an accepted set of transnational practices[10] or a well understood and effective national system of commercial law such that can be used in transnational commerce.

It was and remains the UK's good fortune that English commercial law became in modern times the foremost national system that has met that need. As a result, it has been chosen by business people of many nations (either voluntarily or by participation in a market or by historical

[10] The Hon James Allsop AC (24 April 2024) *The Spirit of the Judicial Task and the Importance of International Judicial Dialogue*, Fifth Full Meeting of SIFoCC, argues that the conduct of international commerce necessitated a law for that activity that could be seen as a distinct system of law, https://cloud-platform-e218f50a4812967ba1215eaecede923f.s3.amazonaws.com/uploads/sites/25/2024/05/SIFoCC-Speech-for-website.pdf.

influence) as the law to govern their transactions even if neither party has anything to do with the UK. It therefore has emerged as a national system that is transnational in its use, because it was and is a system that reflected what commercial people wanted.

2.1.3 The Benefit to the UK

This has been immensely beneficial to the UK economy,[11] as has frequently been pointed out.[12] First, legal services make a direct contribution on 2023 figures of £37bn, having risen more than 60 per cent since 2012; the trade surplus is £7.6bn.[13] Second, 368,000 people are employed in the UK's legal services, two-thirds of whom are based outside London. Third, the UK ranks second in the world for legal services fees. Fourth, there is the indirect contribution that our widely accepted system of law makes by lowering commercial costs and providing the essential basis for economic prosperity and investment. Moreover, there is investment for the future. There are now 356 LawTech companies operating in the

[11] See Oxera Report (October 2021) commissioned by LegalUK, *Economic Value of English Law*, https://legaluk.org/wp-content/uploads/2021/09/The-value-of-English-law-to-the-UK-economy.pdf.

[12] Lord Burnett (2022) *The Hidden Value of the Rule of Law and English Law*, Blackstone Lecture, Pembroke College Oxford, www.judiciary.uk/wp-content/uploads/2022/02/Blackstone-Lecture-2022-final2-1.pdf.

[13] *Legal Excellence, Internationally Renowned UK Legal Services* (10 December 2024), CityUK (CityUK 2024), https://www.thecityuk.com/media/ewkgespt/uk-legal-services-2024-legal-excellence-internationally-renowned.pdf.

UK, 254 of which are UK-founded with investment of more than £1.38bn. The UK is home to 44 per cent of Law Tech start-ups in Europe.[14]

Some complain that there is a 'free rider problem'[15] as people can use English commercial law without having to pay for it. It is said that this makes it hard to calculate the return the UK gets and therefore to find the investment needed to promote English commercial law. This is a complaint that is not easy to understand, as the benefit to the UK from the use of English commercial law is enormous, for so much legal work comes to UK lawyers because of the attraction of the law and dispute resolution under it.

2.1.4 *Is Change a Challenge to That Position?*

It appears on the surface that all seems well for English commercial law. The needs of commerce are undiminished. There is much evidence that English commercial law can be seen as meeting those needs.[16] It has widespread use across the globe. English commercial lawyers have plenty of work and are prospering. Why bother to think about the position? There are a number of reasons why we need to think about the position, but some must be highlighted at the outset – particularly the

[14] CityUK 2024 at page 31.

[15] As explained by David Gauke (3 February 2022) 'English Law Boosts Our Economy So Let Us Promote It Abroad' *The Times*, www.thetimes.com/uk/law/article/english-law-boosts-our-economy-so-lets-promote-it-abroad-p2d3qfoql.

[16] See the scholarly analysis by Philip R. Wood (2022) *Governing Law Risks in International Business Transactions*, Oxford University Press.

current profound changes to commerce and the increasing pace of the development of transnational law.

It might be said there is no problem. Despite the cautious approach taken consistent with the view, expressed by Lord Blackburn,[17] that business people do not like readily to depart from an old practice for fear that a novelty might produce some unforeseen effect, English commercial law has always accommodated change. This can be seen in the development of commerce as people moved to trading worldwide and from sail to steam. In 1886, in the preface to his new work on Charterparties and Bills of Lading, T. E. Scrutton (later Scrutton LJ) wrote:[18]

> The last 20 years have seen what almost amounts to a revolution in the shipping trade. Steamers have supplanted sailing vessels .... The mighty power of steam enables regular voyages to be calculated on, while the large amount of capital invested in a steamer and the keen competition it meets compel the ship owner to take advantage of every hour and minute that can be saved in its employ.

But can we say now there is no problem?[19] The discussion on questions two, three and four posed at the outset of this chapter provides my view of the answer.

[17] *Glyn Mills & Co v East & West India Dock Co* (1882) 7 App. Cas. 591 at page 605.

[18] As cited in Sir David Foxton (2013) *The Life of Thomas E. Scrutton*, Cambridge University Press (Foxton Life of Scrutton).

[19] Hyde (November 2021) *Law and the Open Economy*, Social Market Foundation, at page 30:

> However, developments in technology (including blockchain, additive manufacturing, AI and biotechnology), changing

2.2 Are the Profound Changes to Global Commerce That Commercial Law Faces of a Different Order of Magnitude to That Seen Hitherto?

In addressing the second question, as to whether the changes to global commerce that commercial law faces are of a different order of magnitude, it is helpful first to begin by examining the scale of changes to commerce and then to look at three issues of wider significance.

2.2.1 *The Changes to Commerce*

2.2.1.1 Digitalisation

So much has been said about the effect of digitalisation that it is not necessary to go into detail. Some digital processes such as electronic signatures have had little effect. Although there was some hesitation, it was quickly appreciated that the

commercial patterns (e.g., the growth of digital trade) and the emergence of new business practices (such as concerns for ESG issues, in addition to traditional objectives towards maximising shareholder value) put at risk English law's:

- Capacity for supporting a prosperous domestic economy where these technologies and trends will be central to economic operation
- Popularity as governing law for intentional commercial activity over the coming decades

Consequently, the body of English (civil) law, needs updating across a range of areas, if it is to play a full role in maximising national prosperity.

change could be absorbed into the existing legal regime without much difficulty. As was seen at the start of the Covid pandemic, this greatly facilitated the ability of business to function without the need to obtain wet signatures. The only significant issues related to notarisation, but a practical solution was found. Although many think that smart contracts provide the potential to revolutionise the way business is done by increasing efficiency and transparency, the changes required to commercial law may be few. Because the basic legal framework remains a contract, smart contracts can operate within many existing legal systems. The English Law Commission rightly concluded they can be accommodated within existing English commercial law.[20]

But the effect of other changes has been considerable. I will give four illustrations. First, for many years in Europe a huge amount of scholarly work was expended on drafting a European Contract Code, much of it led by Professor Ole Lando, resulting in the publication in 2008 of the Principles, Definitions and Model Rules of European Private Law – Draft Common Frame of Reference (DCFR).[21] In 2010 those who had expended so much time and scholarship were delighted when the EU Commission decided to use this work as a basis

[20] This was the conclusion of The Law Commission of England and Wales (November 2021) *Smart Legal Contracts, Advice to Government*, https://cloud-platform-e218f50a4812967ba1215eaecede923f.s3.amazonaws.com/uploads/sites/30/2021/11/Smart-legal-contracts-accessible.pdf.

[21] This followed on from the work of the Commission on European Contract Law chaired by Ole Lando, which produced *Principles of European Contract Law* (*PECL*), the last of the three volumes being published in 2003.

for a Common European Sales Law (CESL), which it published in 2011.[22] The draft was a comprehensive attempt to produce a complete code for the law of sales, including remedies, and aimed at business to business as well as to consumer sales. It was hoped, as sales law forms the basis of so much contract law, it could be developed gradually into a code of European contract law. The publication, however, coincided with the start of the market for digital sales.

It was initially thought, as reflected in the published draft, that digital sales could be covered by a few additional paragraphs.[23] As the CESL was being drafted, it became apparent that if it was to operate successfully, then it would have to encompass online sales of both digital products and sales of physical goods. However, this failed to recognise the difference between (1) the purchase of music on a CD or a physical book where the purchaser has the use of that CD or book indefinitely and can give it to someone else and (2) the acquisition of music or an e-book by online download where there is a more restricted right to use; the right to use it usually cannot be given to another person and may only

[22] European Commission, *Proposal for a Regulation on a Common European Sales Law*, 11.10.2011, Com (2011) 635 final.

[23] The Law Commission of England and Wales was sceptical. Its views can be summarised in a key sentence from (2011) *An Optional Common European Sales Law: Advantages and Problems Advice to the UK Government*: 'We think efforts would be better spent on developing a European code for consumer sales over the internet, where there is stronger evidence that the current variety of contract laws inhibits the single market', https://cloud-platform-e218f50a4812967ba1215eaecede923f.s3.amazonaws.com/uploads/sites/30/2015/03/Common_European_Sales_Law_Advice.pdf.

subsist while the person remains in a contractual relationship with the provider. Lawyers distinguish the transactions as falling into different legal categories – sale and a licence to use – but the person acquiring the product would have no reason to appreciate the fundamental legal difference.

The initial view was that the CESL could accommodate in the same broad provisions without much adaptation both forms of transaction by defining sale of goods to include digital products and contracts concluded online. But this proved unworkable. It became very apparent that new thinking was required, particularly as to what modifications had to be made to sales law to cater for digital sales within a single code. Before this could be developed very far, work on the CESL came to an end and progress continued solely in relation to digital transactions. Although the reasons for the abandonment of the CESL were largely political,[24] it proved opportune as digital transactions needed a different approach, though one that could be accommodated within well-established legal principles.

The second illustration is digital assets[25] such as files, records, email accounts, carbon credits, crypto tokens and

[24] Some views are expressed by Professor Hugh Beale, *First Ole Lando Memorial Lecture* (2019) European Review of Private Law 3-2020 [465–486] (Beale Lando) at paragraphs 27–28.

[25] See Law Commission (June 2023) *Digital Assets: Final Report*, https://cloud-platform-e218f50a4812967ba1215eaecede923f.s3.amazonaws.com/uploads/sites/30/2023/06/Final-digital-assets-report-FOR-WEBSITE-2.pdf. Its draft Property (Digital Assets etc) Bill was introduced in the Parliamentary Session 2024–2025 (see evidence given to the Special Public Bill Committee December 2024–February 2025,

non-fungible tokens. All are new but an essential part of contemporary life and commerce. Law is needed to govern access to and the transfer of such assets and how they are to be treated for the purposes of ownership and security and on bankruptcy. A fundamental question that arises worldwide is whether such assets should be treated as property and if so, how, but there is much else that needs to be worked out.[26]

The third illustration is one taken from the new structures that are being brought into existence – decentralised autonomous organisations known as DAOs. These are corporations managed by a decentralised system without a central leadership under which the voting rights to make changes are controlled by 'governance tokens'. DAOs can be used for organisations that run smart contracts or stable coins. These have been set up by those engaged in the industry without worrying too much about their legal nature. Again, this is a worldwide issue[27] and is given sharp focus on bankruptcy.

The final example is banking. Five joint stock banks[28] established dominance in the UK only in 1918, with cheques

https://committees.parliament.uk/committee/746/property-digital-assets-etc-bill-hl-special-public-bill-committee/events/.

[26] See Sir Geoffrey Vos, *The Economic Value of English Law in relation to DLT and Digital Assets* [2023] LMCLQ 48.

[27] The Law Commission of England and Wales (22 November 2022), *Decentralised Autonomous Organisations (DAOs): Call for Evidence*, www.lawcom.gov.uk/project/decentralised-autonomous-organisations-daos/#:~:text=The%20legal%20treatment%20of%20any,used%20to%20create%20smart%20contracts.

[28] Lloyd's, Barclays, Midland, National Provincial and Westminster.

having by then become the dominant means of payment; the first £1m cheque was signed in the Coal Exchange in Cardiff in 1904. The new mechanisms for and the speed of digital payment systems is significantly changing the role of the established banks; it requires legal certainty about the way in which financial instruments that traditionally operated in paper form operate when entirely digital.

2.2.1.2 AI and Automated Decision-Making

AI[29], at this time of profound change where there is no agreement as to its future development, can only get a brief mention, although it is certain that AI will bring about major change to the way things are done in every aspect of life. As generative AI and its application through large language models (or LLMs) develop greater power and capacity at an ever increasing pace and as we must anticipate the advent of Artificial General Intelligence and even

[29] As defined by the OECD (22 May 2019), *Recommendation of the Council on Artificial Intelligence* paragraph 1:

> a machine-based system that is designed to operate with varying levels of autonomy and that can, for explicit or implicit objectives, generate outputs such as predictions, recommendations, or decisions, that influence physical or virtual environments.

https://legalinstruments.oecd.org/en/instruments/OECD-LEGAL-0449. Professor Susskind (2025) in *How to Think about AI*, Oxford defines AI as:

> A branch of digital technology that is devoted to the development and use of systems that can undertake tasks and engage in activities of a sort we have traditionally thought could only be undertaken by humans with our remarkable brains.

'Superintelligence' it is now not easy to predict its precise implications for commerce and the law. Automated decision-making and automated contracting through AI-driven algorithms have already shown that their increasingly sophisticated nature gives rise to legal issues that need to be solved.[30] The most obvious for consumers in respect of automated decision-making is the right to seek human intervention, but there are other legal problems of a more wide-ranging nature that arise in relation to algorithmic contracts. One example is determining which party carries the risk of malfunction of the digital assistant often used in such transactions or incorrect information being communicated or conflicts of interest arising. These are all well-known issues that the law has had to address in other contexts.

2.2.1.3 Climate Change, the Environment and Labour Standards

There is no need to do more than mention climate change, the steps being taken in international supply chains to enforce basic labour standards and the protection of the environment. Again, one illustration will suffice. A transnational market is needed for carbon credits, as these are essential to certain industries such as airlines achieving their climate change obligations. Such a market requires a strong legal foundation,[31]

[30] See, for example, the European Law Institute Interim Report (18 December 2023), *EU Consumer Law and Automated Decision-Making.*

[31] See International Swaps and Derivatives Association (ISDA) paper (December 2021), *Legal Implications of Voluntary Carbon Credits*, www.isda.org/2021/12/01/legal-implications-of-voluntary-carbon-credits/.

which must operate on a basis that works between different nations.[32]

2.2.1.4 Systems Need to Talk to Each Other: Compatibility and Interoperability

The digital age forces us to ensure that systems are compatible – that they can talk to each other. Since the early Middle Ages, traders have used bills of lading to transfer the ownership of goods sent by ship to another nation or to secure the financing of the goods shipped. A standard form was developed across Europe and became worldwide in its use; it was underpinned by law that developed from the practice of using standard formats. For some years there has been a desire to substitute an electronic system for the paper based one. This similarly necessitates systems and laws that are compatible or interoperable.

2.2.2 *The Systems for Resolving the Choice of Differing Laws*

2.2.2.1 The Need for a System

Second, these major changes are increasing the difficulties in resolving which law to apply to a transaction between business people of different nations when they fail to choose a national system or when it is necessary to determine the law that applies to the rights to property of persons other than

[32] See request by ISDA to UNIDROIT in January 2022 to analyse the legal nature of voluntary carbon credits, *Verified Carbon Credits*, www.unidroit.org/work-in-progress/voluntary-carbon-credits/.

parties to a contract. As has already been mentioned, the reason why English commercial law has developed so successfully is either because business people chose English commercial law voluntarily or it was imposed on them by the way in which markets developed so that contracts in wide sections of the world's trade came to be governed by English commercial law.

Where, however, a system of law was not chosen for contracts between traders of different nations, or rights had to be determined that did not depend on an agreement, jurists and courts first began to think of the choice of law from the thirteenth century.[33] A distinction was drawn between procedural law governed by the court of the state and substantive law governed by the law of where the contact was made. This was developed into principles of private international law or conflicts of law that enabled the parties to a transaction and the courts to determine which system of law was applicable.

2.2.2.2 Difficulties with Choice of Law

However, this system has always been subject to a number of difficulties. Mentioning four will be sufficient.[34] When Dicey systematised the principles of conflicts of law in 1896 under the title *A Digest of the Law of England with Regard to the Conflict of Laws*, English law could be briefly expressed as

[33] See M. Wolff (1950) *Private International Law*, 2nd edition, Clarendon Press at pages 21–31.

[34] Professor Hugh Beale sets out a further number including the risk of a court not understanding the foreign law correctly in Beale Lando at paragraphs 9–13.

derived from principles given the paucity of case law.[35] A glance at the current edition of that textbook shows how complex English law on that subject has become.

Second, although a degree of harmonisation was achieved by the EU through uniform laws binding on members of the EU (which the UK has retained), the provisions as to conflict of laws differ from nation to nation.[36]

Third, where the possible applicable laws differ, parties from time to time will engage in what is called forum shopping in the hope of finding a nation whose courts or choice of law will be more favourable to them. One example where this can give rise to futility is differences in the law relating to the interpretation of contracts where some legal systems admit contractual negotiations as evidence of interpretation and others do not. In my experience, save where there is a clear-cut difference in limitation periods or on the kind of damages recoverable, most choice of law disputes

[35] During the evolution of the subject, judges would often cite rules in the textbook as authoritative propositions for their rulings (see, for example, *Singularis Holdings Limited v PricewaterhouseCoopers* [2014] UKPC 36 at paragraph 12 where Lord Sumption said: 'Moreover, while the same rule did not apply to immovable property, the court would ordinarily appoint the foreign office-holder a receiver of the rents and profits: see Dicey, Morris & Collins *The Conflict of Laws*, 15th ed, Rules 216 and 217.' (see now 16th edition 2023)

[36] See Goode Hamlyn Lectures at page 87. In Goode, K & M, at page 17 it is pointed out that the development of national systems of law necessitated the creation of conflicts of law rules; the Hague Conference on Private International Law has adopted a number of private law international conventions.

benefit lawyers and the law rather than commerce and business people.[37]

Fourth, the development of the market in data, digital assets and other emanations of the change in commerce referred to above make the application of conflict rules more difficult in relation to questions that are not determined by a contract. The law that will generally govern rights to property often depends on its location (or as lawyers call it, its 'situs'); it can at once be seen that the location of a digital asset is very difficult to determine, though the Financial Markets Law Committee has suggested a pragmatic solution.[38]

2.2.3 *Rapid Pace of Change and Its Unpredictability*

Added to the significant changes to commerce and the difficulties relating to choice of law, the third aspect of change is its rapidity. This is in stark contrast to the change we have hitherto seen. Another aspect is the unpredictability of the nature of the change as the last ten or so years has shown. For example, as regards AI, no one is prepared to be confident as

[37] James J Spiegelman (Chief Justice of New South Wales, 1998–2111) observed that such disputes were 'always, in all circumstances a waste of money' as cited by his successor Tom F. Bathurst, *The Importance of Developing Commercial Law Systems in Core Values of an Effective Judiciary* (2015) Singapore Academy of Law 176 at page 179.

[38] *Digital Assets: Governing Law and Jurisdiction*, 6 June 2024, https://fmlc.org/wp-content/uploads/2024/06/Report_Digital-Assets-Governing-Law-and-Jurisdiction.pdf.

to how it will affect the law and the interoperability of legal systems, though undoubtedly its effect will be profound.

2.2.4 *The Work of Intergovernmental Organisations in Developing Transnational Law*

Fourth and finally on this second question, there is a step change in the activity of the bodies that make transnational law. However, their role is best understood in the context of the development of English commercial law as the pre-eminent national system of law used transnationally and the development of transnational law that began in the late nineteenth century.

2.3 What Was It That Enabled English Commercial Law to Develop and Adapt So Successfully to Become the Dominant National System Used for Transnational Commerce?

Having addressed the second question by outlining the profound nature of the changes currently facing commerce and commercial law, I can now turn to the third of the questions posed at the outset of this chapter – what was it that enabled English commercial law to develop and adapt so successfully to become the dominant national system of law used transnationally? If English commercial law was able to achieve dominance in the past and maintain it through all the changes, there may be good reason to conclude that it might continue to do so. It is therefore necessary to understand why English commercial law developed so successfully. There are eight factors I would like to consider. Some of the factors that contributed to that success are obvious and can be touched on briefly.

2.3.1 *Political and Financial Stability*

First, and it can be dealt with shortly, is the relative political and financial stability the UK has traditionally enjoyed.[39] Although the people who have exercised political and financial power have changed over the centuries, there has been no political or financial revolution since the seventeenth century. The independent role of the judiciary has remained broadly constant for over 300 years.

2.3.2 *Entrepreneurial Activity and Trading: The Dominance of the UK*

Second has been the huge entrepreneurial, trading and industrial activity across the UK. It was at its zenith the greatest trading and industrial economy and maintained its lead as the greatest trading nation after its industrial economy had been overtaken by Germany and the US.

The markets in which trade developed and was conducted were world markets but also private markets – Lloyd's for insurance, exchanges such as the Baltic for grain and other commodities and shipping and the clearing systems for

[39] See Goode Hamlyn Lectures at page 6 and Acemoglu & Robinson *Why Nations Fail (2012)* Profile Books especially at 305–310.

banking, finance and dealings in futures.[40] The UK was a centre of world commodity markets with their pricing mechanisms and their brokers normally organised for each commodity traded; it was also the world centre for insurance, shipping, banking and finance. In addition, in succession to the chartered companies such as the East India Company, there developed particularly in the nineteenth century the trade associations such as the London Corn Trade Association and the London Metal Exchange with their standards and rules. There were similar bodies for other commodities such as rubber and copra in London and for cotton and wheat futures in Liverpool.[41]

Much has been made of the role of the City of London and in particular the growth of trade, banking and finance, shipping and insurance in the eighteenth century.[42] However, it is necessary to appreciate, particularly in the nineteenth century, the importance of trade and industry across the UK. Liverpool played a significant role as did other cities, such as Birmingham and Cardiff,[43] which the judges visited to try commercial cases. Many of those who were to become great commercial judges began their career out of London; one example was Lord Justice Kennedy.[44]

40 See Goode Hamlyn Lectures at pages 38–42.

41 Sir Ross Cranston (2021) *Making Commercial Law through Practice 1830–1970*, Cambridge University Press at pages 10–11 and 80–81; even as late as the 1930s Liverpool was the leading international market in grain futures, though much smaller than the Chicago Board of Trade, which was confined to US domestic futures.

42 This was traced in Goode Hamlyn Lectures at pages 5–8.

43 See Chapter 1 at page <23>.

44 Sir William Rann Kennedy (1846–1915), www.commercialcourt.london/wr-kennedy#:~:text=William%20Rann%20Kennedy%20secured%20a.

Other important contributory factors were the networks of overseas agents and the centring of communications on London and the fact that sterling was a reserve currency.

2.3.3 *The Role of Judges in Developing the Law and Their Relationship to the Markets*

The third factor is the role of the judges. All three powers or branches of the state – the executive (the government), the legislature (Parliament) and the judicial (the judges) – made their contribution. I will begin with the judiciary as it played the critical role, as in so many areas of law (including criminal law),[45] in developing the law. The judges were by and large supported by the executive and left to do this without much intervention by the legislature.

2.3.3.1 History as the Lineage

It has been traditional to begin consideration of the work of the judiciary by going back to the Middle Ages, though, I should point out some authors, particularly in the eighteenth century, go much further back. I will not do so for two reasons. First, I do not think it can seriously be doubted that transnational commerce has always sought a national system or set of transnational practices that are well understood or accepted; it is not necessary therefore to go back to set out the respective claims of the Code of Hammurabi[46] (who came to

[45] Most of the criminal law was judge made but moderated by a gradual lessening of the severity of punishment.

[46] See Pirie at pages 23–30.

the throne of Babylon in 1793 BCE) or Rhodes (whose Code from the third to fourth centuries BCE was then used by the Romans).

Secondly, so much has been written or recently said[47] about the status of the law merchant or the *lex mercatoria* – a set of customs and usages of merchants. There is the classic and romantic view[48] or 'romantic fantasy'[49] that the law for merchants was confined to its own special courts such as the borough and piepowder courts but in the seventeenth and eighteenth centuries the common law incorporated it. There is the modern view that the common law courts had always recognised the law merchant and the customs of merchants and dealt with cases involving merchants; the difference between the common law courts and those that administered the law merchant was principally procedural.[50] It matters not whether the romantic or the modern view is correct. Just as a nation looks back for a lineage[51]and a sense of history so did the judges of the eighteenth and nineteenth century for their work; for example, Sir James Park[52] set out in 1786 a detailed

[47] See Lord Hodge (October 2022) *The Rule of Law, the Courts and the British Economy* [2023] LMCLQ 34

[48] See, for example, S. Holdsworth (1956) *History of English Law*, vol. 1, Cambridge University Press at pages 526–544.

[49] As described by Lord Briggs (2019) *Mapping the Law in a Borderless World*, 33rd Sutan Azlan Shah Lecture, www.sultanazlanshah.com/pdf/2021/SAS_Lecture_33.pdf.

[50] J. H. Baker, *The Law Merchant and the Common Law before 1700* (1979) 38 Cambridge Law Journal 295.

[51] See Chapter 1 at page <22> in relation to Wales.

[52] Mr Justice Park, known as 'St James Park' to distinguish him from Sir James Parke subsequently Lord Wensleydale, known as 'Green Park'.

historic account of the origins of marine insurance in the introduction to his *System of Marine Insurance*. It is therefore right to begin no earlier than that. It is also unnecessary, as Professor Kadens[53] has pointed out, to explore whether myths of the law merchant give legitimacy to it as a sophisticated legal system created by private groups when not impeded by the intermeddling of the state.

2.3.3.2 Early Trade Practice and Its Adoption

It is simply important to appreciate that commercial law was developed on the backbone of trading in goods: agreeing the contract, shipping the goods, insuring the goods and financing the sale and purchase. In the case of shipping, insurance and financing, the law developed with the heavy influence both as to law and practice from continental or civilian law and practice. The law relating to shipping, Admiralty law, was based on various codes and traditions, the most famous was from Rhodes – the *Lex Rhodia de jactu*, the law of general

[53] Professor Emily Kadens, *The Myth of the Customary Law Merchant* (2012) 90 Texas Law Review 1153; and Sir Ross Cranston, *Theorizing Transnational Commercial Law* (2006–2007) 42 Texas International Law Journal 597 (Cranston) at page 602. Professor Kadens points out that

> Merchants did business face-to-face, and even the Middle Ages had default jurisdictional and conflicts-of-law rules. Furthermore, where foreign merchants gathered, so did intermediaries such as brokers, hostellers, and notaries. These professions existed to mediate differences between buyers and sellers. And when disputes arose, the decision makers may rarely have settled them on the basis of customary rules of decision. Court records instead suggest that most disagreements rested on questions of fact, good faith, and fairness rather than law.

average; some of it came to England via the laws of Oleron (an island in the Bay of Biscay, which passed to the English Crown in the twelfth century through Eleanor of Aquitaine),[54] some through other codes[55] or the practice relating to bills of lading, which was used in very similar form across Europe.[56] Marine insurance and financing through bills of exchange was again devised respectively by merchants in Italian cities such as Pisa, Florence, Genoa and Milan[57] and by Italian money changers.[58] The earliest marine insurance

[54] She had drawn up the laws that Edward III applied in England (see Pirie at page 280).

[55] Such as the *Laws of Visby* (a Hanse Town in the Baltic) and the *Consolato del Mare of Barcelona*, which collected the customs and laws applied in the Mediterranean.

[56] See William Porter Bennett (1914) *The History and Present Position of the Bill of Lading as a Document of Title to Goods*, Cambridge University Press, York Essay Prize 1913. Bennett sets out cases in Court of Admiralty, *Chapman v Peers (1534)*, *The Thomas* (1538) *John the Evangelist (1544)* and *The Brandaris (1546)*, which show that 'by the early 16th century the bill of lading was in the practise of the merchants of Europe a document of title to goods at sea, the assignment or delivery of which to another gave him the right to demand the goods from the master of the ship when she arrived at her port of destination'. It was in a stereotyped form across Europe as is shown by contemporaneous copies of Dutch, French and Italian bills.

[57] See Sir James Park (1787) *A System of the Law Marine Insurance* (Park) at page lxviii; C. Kingston, *Governance and Institutional Change in the Marine Insurance Industry* (2014) 18 European review of Economic History 1 at page 3.

[58] See Benjamin Geva (2011) *The Payment Order of Antiquity and the Middle Ages: A Legal History*, Hart at 354–372; James S Rogers (1995) *The Early History of the Law of Bill and Notes*, Cambridge University Press at 32. Rogers explains how the English law relating to bills of

policies recorded in London were in Italian.[59] They contained a fairly uniform phraseology, which led to a uniformity of practice and interpretation. These passed into English policies of insurance.

The genius (and good fortune) of English commercial law was to take advantage of the growth in the dominance of the UK in transnational trade and its industrial base and adapt the way business was done into a system of English commercial law and to update it to meet economic development that affected the trade in goods and commodities, shipping, insurance and banking. Some consider that the UK was fortunate in this, in contrast to what some view as to what happened in Prussia[60] where hard logic rather than the practice of merchants was the basis of the law.

2.3.3.3 Holt and Mansfield

This adaptation certainly began with two great Chief Justices – Sir John Holt[61] in the beginning of the eighteenth

exchange developed within the common law in response to commercial practice and not by incorporation of the law merchant.

59 Harold E. Raynes (1948) *History of British Insurance*, Sir Isaac Pitman and Sons at page 3; and the colourful account of Italian merchants moving to London and establishing themselves in Lombard Street in Frederick Martin (1876) *History of Lloyd's and Marine Insurance*, MacMillan at pages 17–31.

60 See Goode, K & M at page 7.

61 The practice of merchants in relation to bills of lading adopted in the Court of Admiralty to which I have referred was taken up by the common law courts after the decline of the Court of Admiralty after the Restoration. In *Evans v Marlett* (1696) 1 Lord Raym. 271, Holt CJ said, 'the consignee of a bill of lading has such a property as that he may assign it over . . . and that had been so adjudged in the Exchequer'.

century and the Earl of Mansfield later in that century when its adaptation reached its zenith.

The first task of Holt and Mansfield was to bring order to the law as it had developed. Mansfield maintained a keen eye on commercial practice. He did this through speaking to merchants and businessmen and inviting them to dinner. More importantly, however, he drew on their experience in the courtroom. In *Lilly v Ewer*,[62] for instance, the question arose as to what the term 'sailed by convoy' meant. Did it mean that a ship had to sail as part of a convoy of naval vessels for its entire journey? Mansfield allowed a merchant, Thomas Gorman, to give evidence, but he was treated by Mansfield, as he put it, as no 'common witness'. He was, as we would say today, an expert witness. In that particular case, Gorman's evidence was ultimately rejected as to the meaning of the term. The evidence given by the defendant's 'uncommon' or expert witness was accepted as setting out the proper usage of the term.[63] As Mansfield put it in a related case, 'a great deal must be referred to the usage of

This was confirmed by Lord Mansfield in *Wright v Campbell* (1767) 4 Burr 2046 and in *Lickbarrow v Mason* (1793) 5 T.R. 63, 4 Bro.Prl. Cas 57, by Buller J in his opinion to the House of Lords (set out at 6 East 22n at page 36), commented on by R. S. T. Chorley, *The Conflict of Law and Commerce* (1932) 48 LQR 51 at pages 58–59. See also Charles Abbott (1802) *Law Relative to Merchant Ships and Seamen*, 1st edition, Cushing and Appleton at 173.

62 (1779) 1 Dougl 72.

63 J. Oldham (2004) *English Common Law in the Age of Mansfield*, University of North Carolina Press (Oldham) at pages 134–135.

merchants'.[64] Detail of that usage was the province of the expert witness.

Expert witnesses were not the only means through which the experience of practitioners was drawn into the courtroom. We should not forget that in Mansfield's time civil trials, like criminal trials, were heard before a jury. In commercial matters, there was the facility to hear trials before what was known as a 'special jury', one drawn from experts in the field.[65] Those experts being, for instance, commercial merchants, insurance brokers, traders and so on, their expertise would be practical expertise. In *Lewis v Rucker* in 1761, for instance, Mansfield drew on the expertise of a special jury to enable him to fashion principles of insurance law. As he explained it, the jury:

> understood the question very well, and knew more about the subject of it than anyone else present and formed their judgment from their own notions and experience, without much assistance from anything that passed.[66]

That experience helped form the principles he then went on to articulate in his judgments. In these, and other ways, Lord Mansfield ensured that the judges, and their search for principle, were not divorced from practice. The common law was built upon practical experience and in the result Mansfield developed 'a principled body of law fit to serve

[64] *Hibbert v Pigou* (1783) 3 Dougl 224 cited in Oldham at page 134.

[65] See also Lord Thomas' 1999 Barnard's Inn Lecture: *The Courts of England and Wales, Commercial Education and the Changing Business of the City of London* (2000) 16 Arb Int 141 (Lord Thomas The Changing Business of the City of London).

[66] (1761) 2 Burr. 1167 at page 1168.

the needs of an ambitious and expanding commercial nation'.[67] This approach, while perhaps given its greatest expression by Mansfield, was followed by the great judges of the nineteenth century and thereafter.[68]

2.3.3.4 Support for Markets and Market Practice

This development was only possible because the judges by and large accepted the freedom of those in the markets to contract in the terms and in the way they wanted. The recently published scholarship of Professor Sir Ross Cranston[69] in looking at the archives of commodity markets, trade associations (such as the London Produce Clearing House and the Liverpool Cotton Association), banks, trading houses and manufacturers has shown the extent to which the judges looked to the setting of standards and the making of law by the market, acquiesced in the way the markets worked, upheld the rules of the markets and trade associations[70] – an early form of party autonomy – and upheld a system of self-enforcement through trade association sanctions.[71] One additional benefit was that the judges supported the markets when terms were standardised in the markets in a sophisticated way that reflected the way business people transacted

[67] Lord Bingham's 2005 Maccabean Lecture, *Judges Active or Passive*, given at Cardiff Law School, 139 Proceedings of the British Academy 55 at 61.

[68] Charles Mitchell (2004) Mercantile Usage, Construction of Contracts and the Implication of Terms 1750–1850. In Th*e World of Maritime and Commercial Law, Essays in Honour of Francis Rose* (ed. C. Mitchell and S. Watterson), Hart at page 201.

[69] Cranston. [70] Cranston at pages 31 and 37.

[71] Cranston at page 40.

business; standard terms also achieved a balance and took account of the international character of the market.[72] This way of developing the law also had the advantage that when the judges made decisions the market did not like, then standard terms were altered or clauses devised to reverse the result.[73]

The expansion of industry to distribute and sell overseas drove the development of agency law. The financing of industry and worldwide trade through London as the world's financial centre with its joint stock banking and merchant banking drove the development of law relating to finance; one important example, but of interest in Birmingham,[74] was the development of asset finance by the railway manufacturing companies of the Midlands.[75]

This was accompanied by a restrictive view of public policy[76] and an acceptance of laissez faire epitomised by Lord

[72] Cranston at pages 38–39.

[73] The decision of the House of Lords in *The Inchmaree* (1887) 12 App. Cas. 484 holding a peril was not covered by the standard policy was effectively reversed by the insertion into all policies of the Inchmaree clause; similarly, the decision in *The Coxwold* [1942] A.C. 691 on the wide scope of 'warlike operation' was reversed the Coxwold Amendment, drafted by Sir William McNair: see Donald O'May, *Marine Insurance Law – Can the Lawyers Be Trusted?* [1987] LMCLQ 29. See also illustrations at Cranston pages 358–361.

[74] Where the second of these Hamlyn lectures was given.

[75] By the British Wagon Company and the Birmingham Wagon Company (1852–1963); see Cranston at page 28.

[76] See the examples given by Goode Hamlyn Lectures at page 12: *Rawlings v General Trading Co.* [1921] 1 K.B. 635; *Percival v Wright* [1902] 2 Ch. 421; Cranston pages 39–40 and pages 270–271.

Bramwell's question[77] in upholding the actions of a cartel of shipowners as being lawful – 'What is unfair that is neither forcible nor fraudulent?'

2.3.3.5 The Role of Equity

This is not the occasion to enter into the controversy over the role of equity in the development of commercial law. There is the traditional view expressed by Lord Atkin,[78] when in the Court of Appeal, that introducing equitable principles would dilute certainty. However, the more modern views rightly reflect the reality that equity upheld the need for certainty but performed a valuable role such as that in relation to the fiduciary duties of agents and directors.[79]

2.3.3.6 The Development in Different Markets

Although the judges systemised the principles, they gave pragmatic attention to the needs of specific markets. For example, some twenty years after the decision in *Hadley v Baxendale*[80] establishing the general principle for damages for delay, the rule in that decision was applied to delay in contracts for the carriage of goods by sea in such a way that

77 *Mogul Steamship Company Ltd v McGregor Gow & Co.* [1892] A.C. 25 at page 47.

78 In *Re Wait* [1927] 1 Ch. 606 at 635–636; see Cranston at pages 43–47.

79 See Goode Hamlyn Lectures at pages 17–22; Lord Browne Wilkinson (1995) *Equity and Commercial Law – Do They Mix?*, 10th Sutan Azlan Shah Lecture, www.sultanazlanshah.com/pdf/2004%20Book%201/SAS_Lecture_10.pdf. Lord Milett, *Equity's Place in the Law of Commerce* (1998) 114 LQR 214; Lord Briggs, *Equity in Business* (2019) 135 LQR 567.

80 (1854) 9 Exch 341.

shipowners were in general not liable for damages for loss of market but only for interest on the value of the cargo.[81] It was said that the uncertainties of carriage by sea justified a difference from the ordinary application of the rule, which allowed recovery for loss of market in the event of delay in carriage by land. This was overruled almost a 100 years later in *Heron II*[82] as it had been earlier reversed in the US.

However, the second half of the twentieth century saw successive problems and disruption in the different markets, which enabled the judges to drive the general development of contract law – first the law relating to shipping,[83] then to a lesser extent the grain markets and last of all in that century the insurance and reinsurance markets.

2.3.3.7 No Alsatia: No Refuge from the Application of the Law

But the judges did not absolve themselves completely from maintaining the supremacy of the law. Although there was a general view that the decisions of the market as to practice should be followed and the decision of commercial arbitrators accepted, they would not allow an Alsatia[84] – an area where

[81] *The Parana* (1877) 2 PD 118.

[82] *The Heron II, Koufos v Czarnikow* [1969]1 A.C. 350.

[83] An excellent account of the importance of shipping law, both historically and at the present time, is given in Sir David Foxton's 38th Donald O' May lecture at the Institute of Maritime Law at Southampton University, *Why Shipping Law Still Matters* [2021] LMCLQ 440.

[84] *Czarnikow Ltd v Roth Schmidt & Co* [1922] 2 K.B. 478 at page 488 where Scrutton LJ said of the power of the court to order arbitrators to state a case:

there was a refuge from the law (as there had been in Alsatia, a name given to a small part of London just outside the City between Fleet Street and the river, when in the seventeenth century it became a place of sanctuary and immunity from arrest). If the judges were to enforce awards, then the parties had a right to have the law decided by the judges, a position subsequently changed in 1979.

2.3.3.8 Conclusion on the Use of English Commercial Law

In these circumstances it is not the least surprising that, as the UK was the dominant trading nation and as the judges supported the ways the markets worked though the development of English Commercial law, traders worldwide had to use ways of doing business supported by English commercial law and the standard forms of the English markets and arbitration under them. English commercial law thus moved into becoming the system of national law used transnationally.

> This is done in order that the Courts may insure the proper administration of the law by inferior tribunals. In my view to allow English citizens to agree to exclude this safeguard for the administration of the law is contrary to public policy. There must be no Alsatia in England where the King's writ does not run.

Scots law took a different view: *Sanderson v Armour* (1922) SC (HL) 117 at page 126, but the position in Scotland was changed by the Administration of Justice (Scotland) Act 1972 until the reforms effected through Scotland's adoption of the UNCITRAL Model law on Arbitration by its Arbitration Act 2010. For the change in England in 1979 see Chapter 3 pages 145–146.

2.3.4 *Procedure Developed by the Judges*

The fourth factor is the way the judges developed procedure to provide efficient resolution of disputes. As mentioned, the procedural advantages of the courts of the law merchant were their attraction. Although Lord Mansfield is known best for his development of commercial law, he was also a great reformer of procedure.[85] He also applied reforms to judges too, as he encouraged the giving of oral judgments at the end of the hearing.[86] The need for procedural reform has always proved necessary at various times; the judiciary has played a leading role in achieving such reform.

There was also a willingness to look at other forms of tribunal to hear a case when lawyers and litigants became unhappy with the way the courts were dealing with commercial cases. One suggestion was a tribunal along the lines established for the railways in 1873 – a lawyer chairman with two lay members.[87] Another proposal for which a campaign began in 1852 was for the establishment of Tribunals of Commerce on the continental model where the judges would be merchants. This was rejected by the Judicature

[85] Sir James Park highlights his creation of the representative action so that only one suit had to be brought on a slip with many subscribers, his statement of the case to the jury where he set out the principles and the drafting by the judge of the facts necessary for a special case (see Park at pages xci–xciv).

[86] C. H. S. Fifoot (1936) *Lord Mansfield*, Oxford University Press (Fifoot) at page 36.

[87] Lord Thomas (21 October 2016) *Building the Best Court Forum for Commercial Dispute Resolution*, Wales Commercial Law Association Cardiff (Lord Thomas Cardiff lecture 2016).

Commissioners[88] in 1874. Instead, they favoured the use of assessors along the lines that the Admiralty Court used assessors drawn from the Elder Brethren of Trinity House. This was supported by judges such as Blackburn, Bramwell and Jessel in these terms:

> We are of the opinion that many cases involving for their comprehension a technical or special knowledge cannot be satisfactorily disposed of by the ordinary tribunal of a judge and jury and that the proper tribunal for such cases would be a court presided over by a legal judge, assisted by two skilled assessors, who could advise the judge as to any technical or practical matters arising in the course of their enquiry, and who by their very presence would frequently deter skilled witnesses from giving such professional evidence as is often a scandal to the administration of justice.[89]

But it never proved attractive to those using the courts.[90] Litigants and lawyers did not want it; they preferred the adversarial system of resolving commercial or technical issues through experts. The decision was a significant one because the judges in effect turned their backs on the development of a

[88] Judicature Commission, *Third Report of the Commissioners* (1874) (C.957) at 8–9; C. Burset, *Merchant Courts, Arbitration, and the Politics of Commercial Litigation in the Eighteenth-Century British Empire* (August 2016) 34 Law and History Review 615.

[89] see the power to appoint assessors under Civil Procedure Rules, Part 35.15.

[90] See Lord Thomas, *The Changing Business of the City of London* (2000) 16 Arb Int 141 (Lord Thomas, *The Changing Business of the City of London*).

mixed tribunal for mainstream law[91] and rejected the type of solution that had been adopted for railways.

However, problems persisted. The courts of the late nineteenth century were not for various reasons attractive to business litigants – the introduction of Chancery procedures (such as discovery) after the amalgamation of the courts of law and equity, the cost and the prospect of getting a judge who knew nothing of business (as in fact happened) – but the government and Parliament failed to act. It was solved by the judges creating the Commercial Court in 1895. Much has been written about this,[92] but it is sometimes forgotten that the decision was made collectively by the Judges' Council after a three day debate on 17, 21 and 23 June 1892 on this and other issues such as the need for a Court of Criminal Appeal, a power to deal with lenient sentences and the curtailment of disclosure. A Report and a series of resolutions were sent to the Secretary of State on 1 August 1892.[93] At the same time

[91] They dallied with it again in the 1950s; see Lord Thomas Cardiff lecture 2016.

[92] See Lord Thomas (2018) Keeping Commercial Law up to Date. In *Essays in Memory of Professor Jill Poole* (ed. R. Merkin and J. Devenney), Informa, Routledge; Lord Thomas *The Changing Business of the City of London*; Thomas E. Scrutton LJ, *The Work of the Commercial Courts* (1923) 1 C.L.J. 6; V.V Veeder QC, *Mr Justice Lawrance: The 'True Begetter' of the English Commercial Court* (1994) LQR 292; Sir F. Mackinnon, *The Origin of the Commercial Court* (1944) LQR 824.

[93] Printed in the Law Journal for 13 August 1892 at 526 and presented to Parliament in 1894 (No 27 of 1894); see Lord Thomas, *The Judges Council* [2005] P.L.608 at 614. The Council was chaired by the Lord Chancellor, Lord Halsbury, who at the time had an active and important judicial role sitting in a large number of cases in the House of Lords.

there was powerful judicial support for arbitration, which was immensely strengthened by the establishment of the London Chamber of Arbitration on 29 November 1892, renamed in 1903 as the London Court of Arbitration and again in 1981 as the London Court of International Arbitration.[94]

2.3.5 *Readiness to Look Overseas*

The fifth factor was the readiness to learn and borrow from other jurisdictions, particularly continental.[95] It is right to note at the outset that at times our judges have taken the view that English law should not learn from elsewhere. Lord Camden, when Chief Justice of the Court of Common Pleas,[96] expressed this most firmly in dissenting from a position taken by Lord Mansfield on the utility to be gained from looking to Roman law. He said this about it:

> I am not wise enough to determine which of the two laws is most perfect, the Roman or the English. This I know . . . that almost every country in Europe hath received that body of laws (Roman law), yet they have been with a most stubborn constancy at all times disclaimed and rejected by England. For which reasons . . . I choose to lay aside all that learning as not being relevant in Westminster-hall.[97]

94 V. V. Veeder QC and B. Dye, *Lord Bramwell' Arbitration Code 1884–1889* (1992) 8 Arb Int 329 (Veeder & Dye).

95 American cases also became influential, particularly after the judgment of Cockburn in *Scaramanga v Stamp* (1880) 5 C.P.D. 295.

96 1761–1766. 97 Cited in Oldham at 360.

This was wholly wrong (though there is sometimes a reversion to a belief that the common law has nothing to learn from elsewhere),[98] as another aspect of the genius of the English common law has been to look elsewhere or incorporate other law and the customs and practices of merchants.

Sir John Holt in his judgment in *Coggs v Bernard*[99] adopted a systemisation of the law of bailment (then an important part of commercial law particularly as regards transport) based on Roman law. But it was Lord Mansfield, in his shaping of commercial law, who did not simply draw on the experience of practice to which I have referred[100] but also drew from Justinian, from continental civil law, from the works of Puffendorf, Grotius[101] and Huber. As he put it, for instance, in the case of *Holman v Johnson*, when considering whether a contract could be avoided on grounds of illegality, he decided the issue by noting how:

> The doctrine Huberus lays down, is founded in good sense, and upon general principles of justice. I entirely agree with him.[102]

[98] Lord Bingham's 1991 F. A. Mann Lecture (2000) *There Is a World Elsewhere: The Changing Perspectives of English Law, the Business of Judging*, Oxford University Press at pages 87–102.

[99] (1703) 2 Lord Raym. 909.

[100] See Fifoot at pages 36–37.

[101] N. Poser (2014) *Lord Mansfield, Justice in the Age of Reason*, McGill-Queen's University Press at page 228.

[102] *Holman v Johnson (1775)* 1 Cowp. R. 341 at 344:

> The doctrine Huberus lays down, is founded in good sense, and upon general principles of justice. I entirely agree with him. He puts the general case in question, thus: tit. De Conflictu Legum, vot 2, pag. 539. 'In certo loco merces quaedam prohibitae sunt.

As Professor Oldham describes it, for Mansfield the law was not to be developed by 'ignorance or shortsighted parochialism'.[103] The great English judges of the eighteenth and early nineteenth century in developing the law of marine insurance drew heavily from other jurisdictions;[104] Pothier[105] and Emerigon[106] who wrote in the mid eighteenth century were accorded great respect.[107]

> Si vendantur ibi contractus est nullus. Verurm, si merx eadem alibi sit vendita, ubi non erat interdicta, emptor condemnabitur, quia, contractus inde ab initio validus fuit. Translated, it might be rendered thus: in England, tea which has not paid duty is prohibited; and if sold there the contract is null and void. But if sold and delivered at a place where it is not prohibited as at Dunkirk, and an action is brought for the price of it in England the buyer shall be condemned to pay the price; because the original contract was good and valid.'

103 Oldham at 367.

104 Lord Mustill, *Convergence and Divergence in Marine Insurance Law* (2000) 31 J Mar L & Com 1; J Perillo, *Pothier's Influence on the Common Law of Contract* (2005) 11 Tex Wesleyan L Rev 267 (Perillo).

105 Pothier wrote many treatises on different aspects of the law of contract, the most influential being *Traité d'Obligations (1761)*: see A. W. B. Simpson (1984) *Biographical Dictionary of the Common Law*, Butterworth (AWB Simpson) at page 425.

106 Lord Ellenborough said of his 1783 *Traité d'Assurances*: 'Who has equalled Emerigon as a theoretical and practical writer on the Law of Insurance? He has exhausted every topic, so far as materials were within his reach; and upon all new questions his work, for illustration, and authorities, and usages, is still unrivalled.'

107 Another influential writer was Nicholas Magens who after trading in Spain became English and a director of the Royal Exchange. His *Essay on Insurances* (1755) collected cases and legislation from various cities in Europe.

Although much of this has been forgotten, two of the seminal commercial cases of the nineteenth century drew heavily on continental jurisprudence. In the first of these, *Hadley v Baxendale*, the decision on the limit of damages recoverable from a carrier reflected the approach of the French Civil Code,[108] in turn reflecting Justinian.[109] In the second, *Taylor v Caldwell*,[110] dealing with the consequences of the destruction by fire of a music hall to a contract of the hire of that hall, one of the great nineteenth-century judges, Blackburn J, drew heavily on the French jurist Pothier in setting out the basis of what was to become the English law of frustration. One observation from his judgment will suffice:

> Although the Civil law is not of itself authority in an English Court, it affords great assistance in investigating the principles on which the law is grounded. And it seems to us that the common law authorities establish that in such a contract the same condition of the continued existence of the thing is implied by English law.

However, it was not merely case law that proved of influence but the need for systemisation for which the aid of the executive government and legislature was necessary.

108 See Sir David Foxton (2002) *What Have the French Ever Done for Us? Historic and Prospective French Influences on English Private Law*, Commercial Bar Association Edmund King Memorial Lecture (Foxton King Memorial Lecture).

109 See further Lord Bingham's 2009 Hamlyn Lecture at page 5–6; Perillo at pages 271–276.

110 (1863) 3 B&S 826; 122 ER 309. See Foxton King Memorial Lecture.

2.3.6 *A Sympathetic Executive Government*

The sixth factor was the position adopted by the executive government; for, although the executive government left the development of the law to the judges, it understood the importance of law to commerce.

This can be illustrated in two ways – first, the building of the law courts in London and in the care shown in appointment of judges by the Lord Chancellor. The building of the Law Courts, although funded in large part by the use of the Suitors Fund from the Court of Chancery,[111] saw the Treasury contribute with the strong support of Gladstone to providing a building that reflected the importance of law.

The appointment of Blackburn is a good example of the second. He was still a junior and known more for his law reporting – the eight-volume series known as Ellis and Blackburn – and for his treatise on sale of goods. He was appointed to the Queen's Bench[112] by Lord Chancellor Campbell in 1859 much to the consternation of the profession, which was highly critical of his action in making this appointment.

But this was not always the case. For over twenty years, governments failed to provide a court where judges

[111] David D. Brownlee (1984) *The Law Courts*, MIT Press at pages 65–77; Lord Thomas, Sir Elwyn Jones Memorial Lecture 2004, Bangor University, *The Maintenance of Local Justice* (2003) 3 Welsh Legal History Society 82 at pages 193–204.

[112] He was appointed to the Court of Appeal when formed in 1875 and in 1876 a Lord of Appeal. See E. Manson (1904) *Builders of Our Common Law*, H. Cox at page 258 and AWB Simpson at page 54.

understood the needs of commerce, so the judges, through the Judges Council, as I have mentioned, acted in January 1892 to establish the Commercial Court and the government, through doing nothing, acquiesced.

2.3.7 *The Support of Parliament and Its Non-interference*

The seventh factor was the role of Parliament, which was content by and large to leave business transactions to the markets and, until more recent times, only to intervene to provide help where necessary. As was put very elegantly: 'Mercantile law is very little regulated by statutes and the Acts which relate to it deal for the most part only with isolated points.'[113]

Insurance was a subject that received legislative attention. In the reign of Queen Elizabeth I, a statute was passed[114] to establish a specialist court, the Court of Policies of Insurances, but the courts of common law constrained its use and it fell into disuse. Another example of intervention was the attempts to try and stop insurance being used for gambling, or gaming and wagering, as it was more politely called. At common law policies made without interest were valid;[115] these were expressly prohibited by the Life Insurance

[113] M. Chalmers, *On the Codification of Mercantile Law with Especial Reference to the Law of Negotiable Instruments*, Institute of Bankers, vol. II, March 1881, 113 at 115 (Chalmers Bankers lecture).

[114] 43 Eliz c.12.

[115] *Dalby v India and London Life Assurance Co* (1854) 15 CB 365; *Williams v Baltic Insurance* [1924] 2 KB 282 at 288.

Act 1774[116] and by the Gaming Act 1845.[117] For example, when 'tonners,'[118] contracts of marine insurance that paid out when the total tonnage of ships lost during a year exceeded a set amount, could not be viewed commercially as a form of reinsurance within the marine market, these policies were made unlawful.[119] In 1871 Parliament had to help Lloyd's with private legislation to enable the Committee to exercise discipline over members,[120] but regulation did not come until the 1980s.[121]

Similarly in banking, legislation was needed to enable the establishment and growth of joint stock banks[122]

116 Which prohibited insurance on 'any event or events whatsoever wherein the person ... for whose ... benefit ... such policy shall be made, shall have no interest or by way of gaming or wagering'.

117 Which provided by s.18 that 'all contracts ... by way of gaming or wagering, shall be null and void'. It was taken for granted by the courts and commentators that a purported insurance without an interest at all was to be regarded as a gaming contract within both Acts – see *Wilson v Jones* (1867) L.R. 2 Exch. 139; *Thames & Mersey Marine Insurance v Gunford Ship* [1911] A.C. 529.

118 A transaction that by its very nature contemplates that in many cases the reassured will be seeking a recovery in respect of a loss that he has not suffered and in respect of which he was never at risk is not a reinsurance at all but a bet.

119 S.4 of Marine Insurance Act 1906; Marine Insurance (Gambling Policies) Act 1909.

120 See Charles Wright and Charles E. Fayle (1928) *History of Lloyd's*, Macmillan (Wright and Fayle) at pages 378–382. It arose out of a challenge in the courts to the exclusion by the Committee of a member who had in the view of the Committee acted dishonourably.

121 Lloyd's Act 1982.

122 See the Acts of 1826, 1833, 1844, 1858 and 1862.

and for bills of exchange. The City was otherwise left to self-governance under the Bank of England, which remained a private body until 1946. Statutory regulation came only at the end of the twentieth century.[123]

But similar instances apart,[124] the legislature and the executive government did not intervene until after the First World War, save for some limited codification.

2.3.8 *Systemisation of Commercial Law*

The eighth and last factor was the way the development of commercial law through decisions in a multitude of cases was systematised, particularly by some limited codification and the development of textbooks.

2.3.8.1 The Problem Facing the Common Law

Although there are great benefits in developing a system of commercial law through decisions in cases, its immense drawback is the complexity it engenders. Attempts to address this were made by the compilation of digests of decided cases, but this did not produce any systematisation. Two principal

[123] Banking Act 1979; see Cranston page 37; Goode Hamlyn Lectures page 7.

[124] The Factors Act 1889, which was a consolidation measure of the Acts of 1823, 1825, 1842 and 1877, intended to protect third parties dealing with factors (a mercantile agent entrusted with goods or documents of title). The need for protection arose out of the court's view that the principle of *nemo dat quod non habet* should prevail to protect the owner (*Graham v Dyster* (1817) 6 M.& S. 1).

ways of systemisation were developed – codification[125] and textbooks.

2.3.8.2 Limited Codification: Codify Where the Law Had Become Too Complex

By the time codification was first considered in the UK,[126] there were already in existence the continental codes[127] either directed at those engaged in commerce or directed at certain types of transaction.[128] In contrast, the law of England had to be ascertained from case law. Formidable figures were given; for example, by 1867 it was said the law of England had to be ascertained from about 100,000 cases in 1,300 volumes exclusive of 150 volumes of Irish Reports.[129]

Views against codification were strongly expressed. John William Smith, whose work known subsequently as *Smith's Leading Cases* had so much influence at the time (and later with Lord Denning), predictably had strong views, describing codification of mercantile laws as a 'national

[125] Various definitions of the term are given in Professor Roger Halston, *A Common Lawyer's Perspective on Contract Codes* (2011) 15 Jersey and Guernsey Law Review 150 at 156 (Halston).

[126] Bentham is said to have coined the term in a letter to Tsar Alexander I in 1815, see Halston at 156.

[127] See Professor Johannes W. Flume, *Law and Commerce: The Evolution of Codified Business Law in Europe* (2014) 2(1) CLH 45–83 (Flume).

[128] See Goode, K & M page 8.

[129] In Chalmers Bankers Lecture at 115–116, he cited these figures from the 1867 Royal Commission referred to in the next paragraph and adds that by 1881 the position had been made much worse by the need to look at US cases as in *Scaramanga v Stamp (1880)* 5 C.P.D. 295, Cockburn CJ had commented on how useful US cases were (at pages 300 and 303).

evil'.[130] The impetus to codification therefore unsurprisingly started with an unlikely protagonist, Leone Levi, an Italian who had moved to Liverpool and, when he started his campaign, was not even a lawyer.[131] He compiled in the 1850s a work on commercial law that compared the commercial law of the UK with that of sixty other countries, enlisted Prince Albert and then leading politicians into his campaign and achieved the establishment in 1853 of a Royal Commission to inquire how the mercantile laws of the different parts of the UK might be assimilated.[132] In 1866 a Royal Commission was established to see if the case and statute law of England could be compiled into a digest – a possible way of securing some of the advantages of codification (such as a clear statement of the law within a manageable compass) without the disadvantages of a statutory code that might prove difficult to adapt to changing circumstances. Although the Commission

[130] Smith (1834) *A Compendium of Mercantile Cases* – see AWB Simpson at page 478.

[131] Born in Ancona in 1821, he moved to Liverpool in 1844, was then active in founding the Liverpool Chamber of Commerce, was called to the Bar in 1859 and became a professor at Kings College London; see Annamaria Monti (2021) Leone Levi (1821–1888) and the History of Comparative Commercial Law. In *Common Law, Civil Law, and Colonial Law Essays in Comparative Legal History from the Twelfth to Twentieth Century* (ed. W. Eves, J. Hudson, I. Ivarsen and S. White), Cambridge University Press, pages 236–239; and Lord Rodger of Earlsferry's 1991 Maccabean Lecture, *The Codification of Commercial Law in Victorian Brittain* (1992) 109 LQR 570 at 573 (Lord Rodger) – very much written from the Scottish perspective.

[132] First Report 1854 (P. P. 445); Second Report 1854–1855 (P. P. 1857). However, as the commercial laws of the home nations had derived from the practice and conduct of merchants, there were few differences.

recommended codification,[133] the project failed. However, as was repeatedly pointed out at the time, the UK had failed to codify its law whilst the nations of continental Europe, particularly the German Confederation, had.[134]

One pointed example was that English law on negotiable instruments was estimated to be contained in 35,000 pages of case law scattered across 2,500 volumes of reports, whereas the German law was to be found in some 16 pages of its Code.[135] It was therefore unsurprising that the Association of Chambers of Commerce of the UK and the Institute of Bankers took the first concrete step by requesting MacKenzie Chalmers[136] to draft a law to codify the law for negotiable

[133] Presided over by Lord Westbury. It reported on 13 May 1867.

[134] See Lord Rodger at pages 577–578; Flume explains how France dominated in codification from the sixteenth century; he gives a good account of the 1861 German Commercial Code achieved by the German Confederation through the work of a commission representing the thirty-five then sovereign states of the Confederation between 1856 and 1861. The objective was to provide certainty. It was replaced in 1897 by the HGB, an amended version of the 1861 Code.

[135] As published in Parliamentary Papers (Commercial No 30 (1880) c.2609 – see Chalmers Bankers Lecture at page 120).

[136] He was Standing Counsel to the Board of Trade and became a County Court Judge in Birmingham 1884–1896. Herschell wished to promote him to the High Court, but the reputation of the County Court Bench in the eyes of those who mattered was such as that was not possible – see R. F. V. Heuston (1984) *Lives of the Lord Chancellors 1885–1940*, Oxford University Press at page 113. He then did some work on codification in India, became Assistant Parliamentary Counsel in 1899 and First Parliamentary Counsel in 1902. He was Permanent Secretary of the Home Office from 1903–1908; see AWB Simpson at pages 107–108.

instruments, based on his digest of some 2,500 cases and 17 statutes. His draft became the Bills of Exchange Act 1882.[137] The Sale of Goods Act followed in 1893,[138] reducing more than 1,000 cases to about 60 sections of the Act. Not only was the subject matter of codification limited, but so was its form; each Act was expressed in its long title to be a codification of the law following the advice that it was easiest to get it through Parliament if it did no more than restate the existing law. Different views have been expressed as to why this limited codification was achieved. Some attribute it to the production of the Indian and other colonial codes;[139] some Scots hoped it would be beneficial to their trade;[140] others hoped that codification would proceed on the basis it would unify the laws of the Empire in a grand scheme of imperial codification. However, there was no government or

[137] According to Chalmers in *An Experiment in Codification* (1886) 2 LQR 125 it passed into law because it had the support of Herschell in the Commons and Lord Bramwell in the House of Lords.

[138] The Bill was drafted in 1888 with the assistance of Herschell (then Solicitor General) and Bramwell and introduced in 1889, 1891 and 1892. Part of the delay was caused by the need to consider Scots law so it could apply to the whole of the UK – see Lord Rodger at 581–582; the Scots were enthusiastic that this be done as otherwise they would be left out.

[139] Lady Arden in her 1995 Combar Lecture: *Time for an English Commercial Code* (1997) 56 CLJ 516 as revised in Arden (2015) *Common Law and Modern Society*, Oxford University Press (Arden Combar lecture) at page 201.

[140] Lord Hope, *The Role of the Judge in Developing Contract Law* (2011) 15 Jersey and Guernsey Law Review 10.

parliamentary interest in taking forward such an undertaking[141] as the third and last codification of Chalmers,[142] the Marine Insurance Bill, illustrates.

That Bill was introduced into the House of Lords in 1894, in 1895 and again in 1896. It was promoted by Lord Herschell who viewed it as a codifying bill; it therefore contained no changes to the law. Lord Halsbury (who was Lord Chancellor between June 1895 and December 1905) introduced it again in 1899 and again in 1900. Lord Halsbury again tried for three years to get the Marine Insurance Bill through, but it was blocked in the Commons. By 1901 its prospects were bleak. Chalmers summarised the position:[143]

> Mercantile opinion is in favour of codification, But probably the balance of legal opinion is against it. As long as freedom of contract is preserved, it suits the man of business to have the law stated in black and white. The certainty of the rule laid down is a more important than its nicety. It is cheaper to legislate than to litigate. Moreover, while a moot point is being litigated and appealed, pending business is embarrassed. The lawyer, on the other hand, feels cramped by codification. Discussions on the wording

[141] Lord Rodger at pages 586–587. He concluded that it failed for although businessmen favoured it English lawyers were indifferent.

[142] An attempt was made to codify the law of marine insurance in 1748 based on a Commons Committee Report. The Bill was dropped, many taking the view against codification on the basis it was difficult to make laws to suit every case and seeing their stance justified by the work of Lord Mansfield; see Wright and Fayle at pages 162–164.

[143] *Digest of Marine Insurance* (1901), introduction at page ix (reproduced in 9th edition at page ix) (Introduction to the Digest).

> of the Act in question have to take the place of discussions of principle. No code can provide for every case that may arise, or always use language which is absolutely accurate. The cases which come before lawyers are the cases in which the code is defective. Insofar as it works well it does not come before them. Every man's view of a question is naturally coloured by his own experience, and a lawyer's view of commerce is perhaps affected by the fact that he sees mainly the pathology of business. He does not often see its healthy physiological action.

He therefore produced a digest of the law derived from the work he had done on the Bill. As Chalmers explained,[144] the law of marine insurance was almost entirely common law. There were over 2,000 reported cases but on some points the decisions were meagre and not always satisfactory; some questions were untouched by authority but depended on recognised commercial usage. Chalmers explained many of the older cases depended on commercial conditions that had become obsolete by the end of the nineteenth century. His digest had two objectives (1) to state the main principles of marine insurance law in brief consecutive propositions and (2) to support the propositions where possible by reference to leading cases or cases containing good expositions of principle by eminent commercial judges. His purpose in codification[145] had been (1) to assure the commercial community greater certainty in the law in order to avoid litigation even if this meant an inconvenient rule and (2) to simplify the

[144] See Introduction to the Digest.

[145] AWB Simpson at pages 107–108.

process of legal reasoning by clearly stating the existing principles of commercial law, which hitherto might require distillation from the mass of case law.

When Lord Loreburn succeeded Halsbury as Lord Chancellor in 1905, they both worked together to get the Bill through and did technical work on it. For example, the Commons made twenty-three amendments, which the Lords had to consider on 28 November 1906 in a ping pong. It was finally enacted in 1906. It had taken twelve years despite the fact that at that time Lord Chancellors were lawyers of the first rank as well as being powerful and influential politicians.

There were other attempts. The most illuminating is the attempt by Lord Bramwell to get an Arbitration Code[146] as it demonstrated the strong support of the judiciary for arbitration and the systemisation of law. As subsequently described:[147]

> Throughout its course, the development of arbitration law in England has proceeded by judicial analysis and exposition, in terms of an essentially contractual view of the arbitral process, reinforced by enactment in those cases where the coercive power of the court could not readily be brought into play by simple development of the original agreement to have disputes referred to an arbitrator and to abide by his award.

Bramwell's code was intended to declare the existing state of the law on arbitration in terms intelligible to the

146 See Veeder & Dye at pages 331–352.

147 See Report of the Departmental Advisory Committee on UNCITRAL Model Law [1990] Arb Int 3 (DAC report on UNCITRAL Arbitration) at page 34.

layman;[148] it was introduced in Parliament four times, 1884,[149] 1885, 1886[150] and 1889.[151] It failed, despite strong support from the City, because it could not attract sufficient interest in Parliament; its drafting style encountered the hostility of parliamentary Counsel and the government ended the Bill's prospects by producing its own very limited consolidating and amending Bill, which became the Arbitration Act 1889.

2.3.8.3 The Emergence of Principles in Textbooks

The lack of a codification of other areas of the law fortunately was in large part remedied by the emergence in the late nineteenth century of textbooks. Some take the view that the codifications to which I have referred were a mistake as the law would have been better off without them.

Textbooks were far better. The men who wrote them were remarkable. For example, Judah Philip Benjamin,[152]

[148] Bramwell was assisted by Sir John MacDonnell (then counsel to the London Chamber of Commerce and subsequently Senior Master of the Queen's Bench where he produced the best ever statistics on the business of the courts and Quain Professor of Jurisprudence). He was more scathing than the Departmental Advisory Committee was a 100 years later about the state of the law; see Veeder & Dye page 342:

> It is a serious evil that a law, which laymen in particular are intended to administer and which is designed to diminish the necessity of resorting to the aid of lawyers, should be complicated and not readily intelligible, and should be scattered through many volumes.

[149] Hansard 24 July 1884. [150] Hansard 9 March 1886.

[151] Hansard 28 March 1889 col 997; 6 May 1889 col 1219.

[152] See AWB Simpson at page 43.

after escaping from the US where he had been a Senator and Secretary of State of the Confederacy in the US Civil War, became a barrister on the Northern Circuit and wrote the treatise on sales in 1868; in 1877, he was counsel in thirty out of sixty-five cases reported in the House of Lords law reports for that year. There were books by Dicey,[153] Scrutton[154] and Bowstead,[155] each of whom wrote in the style characterised by short statements of principle (usually called Articles) followed by a discussion of the cases. There can be no better tribute than that of Lord Goff:[156]

> To me, the best code is one which is not binding in law .... The articles which preface each section in such admirable works as [Dicey] [Bowstead] ... constitute excellent and useful epitomes which have the advantage that they need not aspire to completeness; that they may be expressed to be subject to doubt; that they may be changed without legislation; and that judges are at liberty to depart from them if persuaded that it is right to do so.

153 See AWB Simpson at page 148. Dicey is best known for his *Law of the Constitution* (1885). His *Conflict of Laws*, systematised that subject.

154 See AWB Simpson at page 467. T. E. Scrutton's *The Contract of Affreightment as Expressed in Charterparties and Bills of Lading* was published in 1886; it was said he knew this by heart when he practiced as an advocate; See Foxton Life of Scrutton at pages 138–139.

155 See AWB Simpson at page 69. Bowstead's digest of the Law of Agency was published in 1896; he was also general editor of twenty-four published volumes of the *Commercial Laws of the World.*

156 1983 Maccabean Lecture, *The Search for Principle*, Proceedings of the British Academy (1983) 169 (Goff Maccabean Lecture) at page 174.

2.4 How Did English Commercial Law Successfully Engage with the Move towards Creating Transnational Law for Some Aspects of Commerce?

Having considered the third question as to the reasons for the success of English commercial law, I can turn to the fourth question – how did English commercial law successfully engage with the move towards creating transnational law for some aspects of commerce. The last of the eight factors that explains the success of English commercial law provides the setting for one part of that engagement.

The hard fought and desultory efforts at piecemeal codification in England took place in the context of wider moves to codification and a desire to produce uniform principles of law applicable transnationally. It was the clear intention of those from the UK who became engaged in the development of transnational law that it would be based on the soundest of principles – English commercial law. The UK at the highest level of its judiciary therefore played a prominent role in promotion of this work but gradually became more hesitant in accepting and living with the results.

2.4.1 *The UK's Leading Role in the Private International Conferences*

This movement, which sought to create transnational law, began in the second half of the nineteenth century.[157] The UK played a leading role in much of the major work through associations, international conventions, uniform standard terms and, after the First World War, in intergovernmental organisations. I will begin with the associations.[158]

2.4.1.1 The York Antwerp Rules and the International Law Association

One of the first areas of law considered was the law of general average.[159] As I have mentioned, it dated from the third to fourth centuries BCE and passed into the law of European

[157] John Henry Wigmore (best known for his treatise on evidence) in his 1928 *A Panorama of the World's Legal Systems*, West (Wigmore) included in the first twelve chapters a description of legal systems used by specific peoples or nations. His thirteenth chapter, entitled 'The Maritime Legal System' (vol III, pages 875–895) argued that maritime law had been a common legal system by itself for 5,000 years originating as custom but gradually codified and obeyed by all; the Emperor Antoninus had said (Digest, the Lex Rhodia 879):

> I am indeed the supreme lord of the land. But custom is the law of the sea. Let his case be decided by the sea-law of the Rhodians, which our law accepts.

That system had been absorbed into national legal systems with the European codifications in the seventeenth century.

[158] Sir Ross Cranston has examined the extent to which different legal theories explain the emergence of transnational commercial law and its adoption by national systems: *Theorizing Transnational Commercial Law* (2007) 42 Texas International Law Journal 597.

[159] Wigmore saw this as the start of the re-birth of the common law of the sea when changes in commerce after 1830 had brought together shipowners, merchants and insurers in a common desire to override the diversity of national laws that had superseded the original common system of maritime law through the seventeenth-century national codes.

nations. At the beginning of nineteenth century, English practice started to differ from that elsewhere – in Europe where the law had been codified along very similar lines and the United States.[160] After considering pressing for legislation in England and other maritime nations, agreement was instead reached at a private international conference of those who practiced in general average in 1864 at York. Eleven rules were to govern general average and these were to be incorporated into contracts for the carriage of goods by sea, a solution entirely in accordance with the role of private markets in England.

This area of law was then one of the first taken up by the International Law Association (ILA), which was founded in Brussels in October 1873,[161] a month or so after the foundation of the Institut de Droit International. One of the most colourful supporters was the American lawyer and politician David Dudley Field,[162] who achieved the codification of civil procedure in New York and the enactment of a civil code in California and other new states of the US, 'riding with the Codes in his saddle bags' as Professor Grant Gilmore

160 See R. Conrah, *The Road to Vancouver – the Development of the York Antwerp Rules* [2004] 10(2) Journal of International Maritime Law 155–166.

161 His energy was transferred to Europe as one of the founders of Institut de Droit International in Ghent in September 1873 as well as the ILA; see Phillippe Rygiel (2018) *Les Fondateurs de Institut de Droit International* (ed. Francois Chaubert), Presses Universitaires, page 77. It objects were originally aimed at public international law, but the ILA soon engaged in commercial law.

162 Halston at 169–170.

used to declaim in his classes. The creation of the ILA, initially called the Association for the Reform and Codification of the Law of Nations,[163] appears to have been the first time that lawyers had set up an organisation devoted to the advancement of international law. In 1877, at the fifth conference of the ILA at Antwerp, presided over by Lord O'Hagan, the ILA took up work on general average. In 1890 the revised Rules, known as the York Antwerp Rules, were finally agreed at a conference of the ILA in Liverpool.[164]

[163] I am very grateful to Sir William Blair for sight of his brief history of the Committee on International Monetary Law of the International Law Association (MOCOMILA): 1952–2023 given on the occasion of the ILA's 150th Anniversary Conference 2023 held in Paris; see also Mario Giovanoli (ed.) (2000) *International Monetary Law, Issues for the New Millennium*, Oxford University Press; and *About MOCOMILA: Fifty Years of Contributions to International Monetary Law*, Oxford University Press at page v; Lee Buchheit, *An Early History of MOCOMILA*, Notes for the 100th Meeting of MOCOMILA in Berlin, 4–5 September 2015, www.mocomila.org/about/history.pdf.

[164] These in effect reversed the decision of the House of Lords in 1883 in *Svensden v Wallace* (1884) 10 App Cas 404 which took the view that practice developed in England should apply and not be disapplied in favour of the practice elsewhere. Brett MR (later Viscount Esher; see AWB Simpson page 75) had put the 'imperial' position very clearly in the Court of Appeal (1884) 13 QBD 69 at page 73:

> 'I should doubt the expediency of making the law of the greatest commercial and maritime country of the world bend to the law of other countries where commercial operations are far less extensive and where commercial adventure is far more timid ....' The question therefore must be, what is the law of England in this matter.

The ILA was strongly supported by English lawyers and judges. Meetings prior to the First World War were held in London in 1879, 1887, 1893[165] and 1910, in Liverpool in 1882 and 1890 and in Glasgow in 1901. The judiciary and commercial community participated; Lord Justice (William) Kennedy, at one time a judge of London's Commercial Court, was President of the Association in 1899[166] and again in 1908 to 1910; Lord Phillimore was President from 1905 to 1908;[167] Lord Porter in 1946. There were others, including Walton J who chaired a committee of the ILA on general average; Pickford LJ who, as Lord Sterndale, was an active member of a more specialist body, the Comité Maritime International (CMI) and chaired the House of Lords Committee that reviewed the incorporation of the Hague Rules; and MacKinnon J who participated in the work of the CMI on the Hague Rules.[168] The international outlook was reflected in the speech of the then Lord Mayor[169] who, in welcoming the ILA in 1893, said:

[165] For the report of this conference, see, https://archive.org/details/reportconferenco6confgoog/page/n8/mode/2up.

[166] See his address to first meeting held outside Europe in Buffalo that year, https://archive.org/stream/reportsfirstcono2assogoog/reportsfirstcono2assogoog_djvu.txt.

[167] Walter Phillimore, Lord Phillimore of Shiplake – the commercial court of England & Wales.

[168] Sir Joseph Walton – the commercial court of England & Wales; William Pickford, Lord Sterndale – the commercial court of England & Wales; Sir Frank MacKinnon – the commercial court of England & Wales.

[169] Alderman Sir Stuart Knill Bart.

> The codification of the laws of nations in connection with commerce, and more particularly in connection with the mercantile marine, must have the full sympathy of every one engaged in commerce in this country, and especially in this City.[170]

The tortuous journey to achieve the codification of English marine insurance law was paralleled with an attempt to get some international uniformity on marine insurance. T. G. Carver QC[171] presented a paper at the ILA conference at Buffalo in 1899[172] urging that to progress international commerce an attempt should be made to devise a set of uniform rules for marine insurance, but confined to those areas where the law differed (particularly constructive total loss, the effect of unseaworthiness and negligence and double insurance). It did not succeed.

2.4.1.2 Comité Maritime International

The ILA tried at and after its conferences in 1882 at Liverpool, in 1885 at Hamburg and in 1888 at Brussels to make progress with producing a uniform bill of lading, as nations other than the UK, whose maritime commerce dominated the world, wanted an international agreement that more broadly

[170] See report at page 30.

[171] Subsequently Judge Carver. He had published the first edition of *Carriage of Goods by Sea* in 1885. His name is preserved, like Benjamin, in the title of two twenty-first-century treatises published by Sweet &Maxwell: *Carver on Bills of Lading* and *Carver on Charterparties*.

[172] Report of the Conference at page 103, https://archive.org/stream/reportsfirstcon02assogoog/reportsfirstcon02assogoog_djvu.txt.

reflected the laws of other nations. As reported in the ILA conference in London in 1893:[173]

> It has occupied the attention of our meetings ever since 1882, when the first attempt was made at Liverpool to form a bill of lading which might satisfy the wants of the commercial world.

As the ILA had other matters that caught its attention, the CMI, which had been established as a private body in Antwerp in 1897, developed out of the ILA with the specific objective of the unification of the principles of maritime law through drafting international conventions[174] and performing other tasks such as taking custody of and responsibility for the York Antwerp Rules. The way in which the CMI worked was to prepare draft conventions that were submitted to the Belgian government, which then convened diplomatic conferences to agree the conventions. The most well-known of these was the uniform rules applicable to bills of lading, the Hague Rules 1924, which were incorporated into the laws of most nations under Carriage of Goods by Sea legislation.

English judges and lawyers, including Sir Henry Duke P., Lord Phillimore, Maurice Hill J. and Sir Leslie

[173] See page 33 of the Report.

[174] See Birch-Reynardson, *The CMI (1983)*, https://comitemaritime.org/wp-content/uploads/2018/06/past-achievenemts.pdf; and Michael F. Sturley (ed.) (1990) *The Legislative History of the Carriage of Goods by Sea Act and the Travaux Preparatoires of the Hague Rules*, Fred B Rothman & Co, Colorado (*HR Travaux Preparatoires*), vol 1 at page 5.

Scott,[175] participated in this work on bills of lading both before and after the First World War. However, in the result some including two of the most prominent commercial judges, Lord Sumner and Scrutton LJ, were hostile to the Hague Rules.[176] Their view was that the Hague Rules struck at freedom of contract. Both were bitterly critical of the drafting, which they thought would give rise to uncertainty and endless litigation. This would undermine what the judges had achieved, as it was in sharp contrast to the clarity of the law that had emerged when there was freedom of contract. Their opposition to the Hague Rules, however, failed. That was in part because of the decline in the power of British shipowner interests after the First World War and in part because of pressure from other nations (which had resulted in legislation in the US, Australia and Canada) and from those

[175] In May 1921 a conference of the ILA's Maritime Law Committee under the presidency of Sir Henry Duke had agreed to formulate model rules for bills of lading. He presided over further conferences in 1921 in the Hague and in London in October 2022, which was also attended by Lord Phillimore and Sir Maurice Hill (another judge of the High Court) (see vol. 2 of HR *Travaux Preparatoires*). The UK delegation to the Diplomatic Conference later in October 1922 and in 1923 in Brussels was led by the Solicitor General, Sir Leslie Scott KC (*HR Travaux preparatoires*, vol. 1, pages 343, 423); he had begun his commercial practice in Liverpool and was subsequently appointed to the Court of Appeal in 1935 at the age of sixty-six. The Presidents of the conferences in England, which discussed this at an earlier stage had been Sir Walter Phillimore in 1899 and Sir Willaim Kennedy in 1905.

[176] See *HR travaux preparatoires* (see Lord Roskill's review at (1992) 108 LQR 501 and Report of the Joint Committee on the Carriage of Goods by Sea Bill paper 106 and the Imperial Shipping Committee Report Cmd 1205).

who shipped goods by sea, who resented the monopoly power of shipowners through their cartels. These judges were also, in the view of the Select Committee of Parliament, quite wrong about the drafting of the Hague Rules.[177] In the result, the view of the Select Committee about the drafting was correct and that of the judges wrong.

2.4.1.3 The Hague Conference on Private International Law (HCCH)

In 1893 Tobias Asser, a Dutch lawyer who was one of the founders of the Institut de Droit International, also founded the Hague Conference on Private International Law (which came to be known as HCCH),[178] which began work on the unification of private international law. Six sessions were held between 1893 and 1928. In 1896, it published the first Hague Convention, the Convention on Civil Procedure; the other conventions were on family law.

2.4.2 *Use of Standard Forms and the Subsequent Influence of the ICC*

In contrast to the active engagement in these international associations was the fostering of the use and influence of standard form contracts, which, as mentioned earlier, had developed in the English markets. Many of these provided for arbitration in London; as this carried with it the right to go to the Court, it provided many opportunities for the judges to

[177] See paragraphs 17–19 of the Report; the Committee paid tribute to the work of the British Representatives, Sir Norman Hill and Mr Andrew Jackson.

[178] Hague Conference, Conférence de la Haye.

develop the law. The influence of these standard terms over time was substantial. As Lord Goff put it so elegantly:

> In a sense, we do not have one Commercial Code but several, to be found in all the standard forms so widely used throughout the world - the Lloyd's form of standard marine policy, the various forms of charterparty and commodity trade contract, and so on.[179]

In the field of marine insurance, for instance, English standard terms became dominant. In 1978 a Report noted that

> despite the variety of national marine insurance policy conditions, it may be said that the use of the policy forms produced by the English insurance market for both hull and cargo insurances . . . have become so widespread that the policy forms are virtually de facto international insurance conditions. Approximately two thirds of the countries in the world utilising hull and cargo insurance respectively use the English conditions solely, as an alternative to, or sometimes in conjunction with, local policies. When considering only developing countries, this figure rises to about three quarters.[180]

[179] Lord Goff of Chieveley, opening address, second annual JCL conference in London on 11 September 1991 (1992) 5 Journal of Contract Law 1 at 3 cited by Gerard McMeel (2020), Are There Any General Principles of Contract Law? In Th*e World of Maritime and Commercial Law, Essays in Honour of Francis Rose* (ed. C. Mitchell and S. Watterson), Hart at page 181.

[180] UNCTAD Marine Insurance. TD/B/C.4/ISL/27 20 November 1978, paragraph 45; repeated in the 1982 revision of the report, https://unctad.org/system/files/official-document/c4isl27rev1_en.pdf

The dominance was explained in the Report[181] as the result of the historic economic predominance of the London market, the high level of expertise in the English market and the importance of established precedent. Once policy conditions became widely used and understood, increased use of them was self-generating as insurances on such terms were more readily accepted. A striking example of the widespread usage of the terms is that in the 1980s the insurance to be provided for NATO fleets by the Interallied Insurance Organisation, a NATO Civil Wartime Agency, in the event of the outbreak of a ground war in Europe with the Soviet Union, was be on the terms of the London market.

However, in banking there was a marked change in one market through the work of the ICC, which was established in 1919 in Paris. Amongst its activities were and are the production of uniform terms to be incorporated into agreements. Two of the most important of the ICC's standard terms are the Uniform Customs and Practice for Documentary Credits (UCP) applicable to letters of credit (first published in 1933[182] and revised many times) and the Uniform Rules for Demand Guarantees (URDG) applicable to demand guarantees (first published in 1991). These terms take effect by being incorporated into the agreements undertaken by banks when providing letters of credit or demand

[181] Which noted that terms developed by ILA in 1901 known as the Glasgow Insurance Rules (as they were drafted at the 1901 conference in Glasgow presided over by Lord Alverstone, then the LCJ of England) never obtained wide acceptance.

[182] EP Ellinger [2007] LMCLQ 153.

guarantees. They have entered into standard use worldwide and provide in effect transnational terms.

The need for such uniformity in banking is illustrated by what happened in 1951 when the British banks declined to accept a revision made to the UCP. From then until 1963, there were two different practices – that of the UK followed by much of the Commonwealth and the 1951 revision to the UCP followed by the rest of the world. Although it brought business to London, it was very inconvenient to the progress of multinational banks. A further revision was agreed in 1963 and then adopted by all.

2.4.3 *The Role of the Nation-State in Intergovernmental Conferences and Organisations*

After the First World War, intergovernmental bodies where the state acted as the sponsor were established. These gradually assumed a primary role in place of the private organisations that had been formed in the nineteenth century.

UNIDROIT (International Institute for the Unification of Private Law) was established in 1926 as an auxiliary organ of the League of Nations based in Rome with the objective of harmonising private law with an emphasis on commercial law. It has produced important international principles, particularly its Principles of International Commercial Contracts, and international agreements.

In the post-war era, HCCH was transformed in 1951 into an intergovernmental organisation alongside UNIDROIT in its seventh session – there having been no sessions since 1928. Its sole language was French until 1964 when English was adopted as the second official language to facilitate the participation of more common law countries.[183] Much of the work was on family law and in 1998 the International Hague Network of Judges was established to promote direct judicial cooperation between judges in family law in which England has played a leading role. Three conventions important to commercial law were the Choice of Court Convention 2005, the Principles on Choice of Law in International Commercial Contracts 2015 and the Judgments Convention 2018.

In 1964 the UN established UNCTAD[184] with a view to using international trade to promote economic development of the less developed nations. The developing nations dominated as there were ninety, as opposed to the thirty developed nations. In 1966 UNCITRAL, the UN Commission on International Trade Law, was formed to play a more active role in reducing or removing disparities in national laws governing international trade that created obstacles to the flow of trade. UNCITRAL has produced international conventions, agreements on uniform law between nations that become binding as the law of each state on ratification. The most successful of the conventions has been the 1980 UN Convention on Contracts for the International Sale of Goods 1980 (CISG) ratified by ninety-five nations but

[183] HCCH, *History*, www.hcch.net/en/about/history.

[184] M. Daunton (2023) *The Economic Government of the World*, Allen Lane at pages 415–426.

not the UK.[185] UNCITRAL also produces model laws. These do not take effect as uniform laws under international agreements but are model provisions of law each state can use to make its own law conform to a uniform international standard. One of the best known is the Model Law on Arbitration agreed in 1985, but again not adopted by England, though it was by Scotland.

All of these transnational bodies are now engaged in creating legal regimes to govern the changes to commerce I outlined at the outset. Attempts are made to coordinate this work as can be seen from UNCITRAL, HCCH and UNIDROIT's 2020 Legal Guide to Uniform Instruments in the Area of International Commercial Contracts, with a Focus on Sales.[186] However, progress is slow but improving.[187]

2.4.4 *The New* Lex Mercatoria *or New Law Merchant*

There is one final matter to mention. In the second half of the twentieth century there was a revival of interest in the law merchant or *lex mercatoria* under the influence of Professors

185 The UK representatives included Professor A. G. Guest the then general editor of the newly recreated Benjamin on Sale of Goods.

186 UNICITRAL, *Legal Guide to Uniform Instruments in the Area of International Commercial Contracts, with a Focus on Sales*, https://uncitral.un.org/sites/uncitral.un.org/files/media-documents/uncitral/en/tripartiteguide.pdf.

187 For a 2023 view, see Sir Roy Goode (2023) Transnational Commercial Law and Impediments to Its Development. In *Shaping the Law of Obligations, Essays in Honour of Ewan McKendrick* (ed. Peel and Probert), Oxford University Press.

Berthold Goldman, Clive Schmitthoff and Peter Berger and other legal scholars[188] in what has come to be termed the new *lex mercatoria* or the new law merchant.[189] This comprises a set of general principles[190] said to result from globalisation and to be applicable to transnational commerce where national law might not provide the answer. The principles are seen either as an autonomous system of transnational law derived from general commercial custom or practice, or general principles common to national systems, or from the contract between the parties irrespective of the national law governing the contract. Although some courts have drawn on decisions of courts of other nations in resolving questions, most courts have till now always approached this task as assistance in determining national law rather than identifying self-standing or autonomous transnational law.

Conclusion: The Achievement, the Weaknesses and the Benefits

The achievement of English commercial law has been considerable in providing a system of law with numerous strengths

[188] Sir Ross Cranston, *Theorizing Transnational Commercial Law* (2007) 42 Texas International Law Journal 597 at 601–607.

[189] See Lord Mustill (1987) The New *Lex Mercatoria*: The First 25 Years. In *Liber Amicorum for Lord Wilberforce* (ed. M. Boss and I. Brownlie), *Clarendon Press* at pages 149–183. Goode, K & M at pages 23–32.

[190] Lord Mustill identified twenty such principles (see page <xx>), but Professor Peter Berger's CENTRA, a research facility at the University of Cologne has developed a much more extensive set of principles published at www.trans-lex.org/principles/of-transnational-law-(lex-mercatoria).

widely accepted as a national system of law for transnational commerce. In this achievement, English commercial law provided and continues to provide a national system of law that enables transnational business to be conducted effectively, at a reasonable cost and with good assurance as to the risks. Its certainty is demonstrated when it matters most particularly on insolvency. In short, it has become and continues to be the dominant national law used for transnational commerce in many areas of commerce.

However, it is clear from the profound changes to commerce that were outlined earlier and from the development of transnational law that there is a need to examine the future use of English commercial law as a national system used for transnational commerce. In addition, account must be taken in that examination of the UK's loss of trading dominance and real competition from other nations both in the attractiveness of their law and their systems for resolving disputes.

In the wider terms of Miss Hamlyn's objective in establishing these lectures, it is right also to conclude that the UK undoubtedly has had and continues to derive great benefits from the strength of English commercial law. However, given the significant changes that are currently occurring, is there the will, ability, vision and capacity to think radically to build on those foundations? We need to be able to fulfil our responsibilities and obligations particularly for the benefit for the future generations. Chapter 3 turns to examine whether English commercial law's current dominant position in transnational commerce can be maintained so that it remains the main foundation for the continued development of transnational commerce.

3

The Development of Transnational Law for Commerce and the Continuing Role of English Commercial Law

Chapter 2 concluded by asking the question that this chapter seeks to answer: Can English commercial law's current dominant position in transnational commerce be maintained so that it remains the main foundation for the continued development of transnational commerce? This will need the will, ability, vision and capacity to think radically and it will need leadership.

In this chapter, I consider that issue by asking four specific questions

1. What are the advantages English commercial law retains?
2. What are the issues facing English commercial law?
3. What are the options for enabling English commercial law to maintain its position?
4. What conclusions can be drawn on the future of the law for transnational commerce?

3.1 What Are the Advantages English Commercial Law Retains?

The starting point must be an overview of the current position English commercial law has attained for the reasons explained in Chapter 2. What are the advantages it retains and the issues it faces?

3.1.1 *The Strengths of English Commercial Law*

It is important to state at the outset that there has been no diminution in the attraction of English commercial law as a national system of law that enables transnational business to be conducted effectively at a reasonable cost with a good assurance as to the risks. Its strengths can be summarised as:

1. Allowing freedom of contract by leaving so much to the markets and, save where constrained by statute, adopting a laissez faire approach.
2. Providing certainty[1] and predictability as to the outcome.
3. Holding parties to their bargains, even if harsh. A clear example of this was allowing a shipowner to benefit from a rising market by withdrawing a vessel from a charter when payment was late due to an error in the transmission of payment.[2]
4. Providing at times flexibility to meet commercial expectations[3] or adaptability, which is necessary for the

[1] See, for example, *The Scaptrade* [1983] Q.B. 529 at 540–541 (Rober Goff LJ); *Bank Line v Arthur Capel* [1919] A.C. 435 at 454; *The Golden Victory, Golden Strait Corporation v Nippon YKK* [2007] UKHL 12.

[2] See *Tankexpress v Cie Financiere Belge* [1949] A.C. 76; the House of Lords made clear in *The Scaptrade* [1983] 2 A.C. 694 that there would be no relief under the equitable principle of relief from forfeiture.

[3] See, for example, *Embiricos v Sydney Reid* [1914] 3 K.B. 45 at page 54 (Scrutton LJ).

development of the law to keep pace with industrial and commercial change.

5. Serving the market through understanding commercial practice and giving effect to it, as has been often explained,[4] for example, by Lord Steyn,[5] Lord Goff[6] and Lord Devlin.[7] Sometimes this has been done in circumstances that may have been legally dubious.[8]
6. Being adept in making rudimentary agreements work; an example is the acceptance of the slip at Lloyd's and elsewhere in the London insurance market as a workable contract of insurance, even if no policy was issued.[9]

[4] Though sometimes contested: R. S. T. Chorley, *The Conflict of Law and Commerce* (1932) 48 LQR 51; and Foxton Life of Scrutton at pages 270–272.

[5] Lord Steyn, *Contract Law: Fulfilling the Reasonable Expectations of Honest Men* 11th Sultan Azlan Shah Lecture (1996), www.sultanazlanshah.com/pdf/2004%20Book%201/SAS_Lecture_11.pdf, as revised and published at (1997) 113 LQR 433.

[6] Lord Goff, *Commercial Contracts and the Commercial Court* [1984] LMCLQ 382. Custom and usage so important to the development of the law in earlier centuries is of little importance today; recourse to its use today is non-existent as the requirements set out in *Kum v Wah Tat Bank* [1971] 1 Lloyd's Rep 439 are so high and its disuse is beneficial as it was difficult to overrule a usage recognised by a court.

[7] Lord Devlin, *The Relation between Commercial Law and Commercial Practice* (1951) 14 MLR 249.

[8] See the two cases in relation to the 'practice' in London not to regard the arbitration clause in a charterparty on the Centrocon Form to be incorporated into a bill of lading when the other terms of the charter were. *The Njegos* [1936] P. 90 and *The Annefield* [1971] P. 168. See also Cranston at pages 52–56.

[9] The problems that arose were in relation to stamp duty; see Wright and Fayle pages 289–293; see Park at pages 39–40.

7. Being prepared to borrow from other systems in substantive and procedural law as the judges did in creating the *Mareva* or freezing injunction based on *saisie conservatoire*[10] or adapting approaches to interpretation to accommodate the terms of transnational instruments.[11]
8. Facilitating law reform to protect English commercial law and the business of the courts. For example, the judges led by Lord Diplock[12] took the view that the interests of commerce and arbitration in London were not served by reserving to the judges all issues of law. They promoted the reform that allowed contracting out of any review by the judges on grounds of substantive law. They contended that the well-established approach of allowing judges to intervene to correct and develop the law was out of step with other arbitration centres. It was, they believed, making London a less attractive prospect for dispute resolution. London had an excellent commercial law, but there was a need, in their view, to make London an equally excellent forum for dispute resolution through arbitration. To achieve this, London, it was argued, would have to change the approach so that there was greater finality

[10] See Lord Bingham (2000) *The Business of Judging*, Oxford University Press (*Business of Judging*) at 97–98, though there is always the need to update as shown by *Broad Idea International Ltd v Convoy Collateral Ltd* [2021] UKPC 24.

[11] See Bingham MR on the approach to the interpretation of the UCP in *Glencore Internation v Bank of China* [1996] 1 Lloyd's Rep 135 at 148, followed and amplified in *Fortis Bank SA v Indian Overseas Bank* [2011] EWCA Civ 58 at paragraph 29.

[12] Lord Diplock, *Alexander Lecture*, Arbitration (1978) 44(3) 107, thus reversing the position as discussed in Chapter 2 at pages 104–105.

and certainty in arbitral awards. The reform was effected in two stages,[13] first by Parliament and then by the interpretation by Lords Diplock and Denning[14] of the provisions of the statute enacted by Parliament.[15]

13 The Arbitration Act 1979. The Act replaced the special case by a right of appeal with leave to the court and with the right to contract out of the right of appeal save in restricted categories of case.

14 The Act was, however, open to two interpretations: (1) that the court would give leave where there was a real and substantially arguable point of law or (2) it was much more restrictive. The issue arose in *The Nema (Pioneer Shipping v BTP Toxide)* [1980] Q.B. 547, [1982] A.C. 724 where the issue was whether a charterparty had been frustrated on which an urgent decision was needed. It therefore provided the right occasion for the second view to prevail both in the Court of Appeal and in the House of Lords; that was because the issue of frustration is sometimes treated as a mixed question of law and fact and an urgent decision was needed. In the Court of Appeal, Lord Denning went so far as expressing the view that a commercial arbitrator was more likely to be better placed to interpret the contract in a commercial sense than a judge and in a one off case probably more likely to be right than a judge, see [1980] QB 547 at 564–565. Before the case reached the House of Lords, a very great commercial judge, Robert Goff J (later Lord Goff) pointed out in *Schiffahrtsagentur Hamburg Middle East Line GmbH v Virtue Shipping Corpn (The Oinoussian Virtue)* [1981] 2 All E.R. 887; [1981] 1 Lloyd's Rep. 533 in unanswerably correct terms the fallacies in the approach of Lord Denning. It was to no avail. In the House of Lords, Lord Diplock set out guidelines for the very strict approach by what was clear judicial legislation implementing the ideas that he had foreshadowed in his Alexander lecture.

15 In the Fourth BAILII lecture, *Developing Commercial Law through the Courts: Rebalancing the Relationship between the Courts and Arbitration*, which I gave in 2016, I was very critical of the effects of this change, www.judiciary.uk/wp-content/uploads/2016/03/lcj-speech-bailli-lecture-20160309.pdf.

9. Being willing to listen. One of the most important strengths of English commercial law is the ability of courts to admit they got the law wrong. In 1974, the House of Lords gave a decision in the *Aello*[16] on a laytime clause allocating the risk of delay to a ship when waiting at an anchorage before entering a port. It was refreshing when Roskill LJ said in the Court of Appeal in the *Johanna Oldendorff*[17] in relation to that decision:

> It is widely known that it was not a popular decision in St Mary Axe or the Temple. It is also widely known that its application has from time to time caused difficulty not only to brokers and umpires but also to judges

Lord Diplock was more direct:

> The effect of the interpretation adopted by the majority [in the *Aello*] . . . was to substitute for what had previously been understood to be the criterion for the commencement of laytime a different criterion, which experience has shown to lack precision and to have little relevance to the business nature of the adventure.
> In consequence how it will apply if delay due to congestion should occur at any particular port has become unpredictable.[18]

The House of Lords accepted the error and overruled the *Aello*.

[16] [1961] A.C. 135. The commercial background on the allocation of risk is set out in the judgment of Lord Diplock in *The Johana Oldendorff* at pages 553–555 and at page 556.

[17] [1974] A.C. 479 at page 513.

[18] [1974] A.C. 479 at page 555.

10. In continuing to innovate. One illustration is the establishment of the Financial List and its test case procedure, which was so important in the rapid resolution of the business interruption cases arising out of the Covid emergency – the case started in the High Court on 9 June 2020 and the Supreme Court delivered its judgment on 15 January 2021.[19]

In short, English commercial law provides a national system of law that enables transnational business to be conducted effectively, at a reasonable cost and with good assurance as to the risk. Its certainty is demonstrated when it matters – on insolvency. It continues to be the dominant national law used for transnational commerce in many spheres such as shipping and of significant importance in financial and derivative transactions.

3.1.2 *English Courts and English Arbitration*

Nor has there been any diminution in the attraction of and the trust in the judges in the UK. Continued confidence in the strength and specialism of the judiciary in its decisions and in its development of English commercial law is as great as ever.[20]

[19] *Financial Conduct Authority v Arch Insurance (UK) Ltd* [2021] UKSC 1. See Civil Procedure Rules Part 63A and PD63A paragraph 6.

[20] The figures for 2023 are at City UK 2024 at pages 37–44.

The fact that at times judges take bold courses is important. Lord Donaldson,[21] for example, did so in one of the first of the cases arising out of the troubles at Lloyd's in the autumn of 1979;[22] he adjourned a summons in the Commercial Court and heard it at Lloyd's as he took the view that the reputation of the market would be seriously damaged by the litigation and Lloyd's had to find a solution. His actions ensured arbitration was considered, taking the immediate pressure off Lloyd's and the proceedings were eventually settled.

The position of London as a seat of arbitration remains strong[23] with the excellence of many of its arbitrators recognised worldwide[24] as is the standing of the London Court of International Arbitration established in 1892. The structure developed in the nineteenth and twentieth centuries supported physical markets as well as giving rise to futures

[21] His account of the working of the Commercial Court given in the 7th Sutan Azlan Shah Lecture (1992) shows his approach to dispute resolution, https://www.sultanazlanshah.com/pdf/2004%20Book%201/SAS_Lecture_7.pdf (Lord Donaldson's Sutan Azlan Shah lecture)

[22] Claim by Names against Sasse Syndicate at Lloyd's in which the names sought an injunction against the Committee of Lloyd's preventing them paying claims under insurances written under a binding authority granted by Sasse to agents in the US. A fairly accurate account of this is set out in Godfrey Hodgson (1984) *Lloyd's of London: A Reputation at Risk*, Allen Lane at 274–275.

[23] *Law Commission Review of the Arbitration Act 1996: Final Report and Bill* paragraph 1.4, September 2023; CityUK 2024 pages 45–46.

[24] There is less use of one of the great strengths of English arbitration – a tribunal of two familiar with the trade or business in issue in the arbitration and a lawyer chairman. For the establishment of the London Court of Arbitration in 1892, see Chapter 2 page 109.

and derivatives markets. Despite the demise of most of the physical markets, the structure remains with the benefit of their standard form contracts providing for English commercial law and their provisions for arbitration in London.[25] Some offer a choice of law or arbitration venue,[26] but English commercial law and London are holding their own.

3.1.3 *The English Language*

Gradually English has consolidated its position as the language of business and the law over the past thirty years.[27] It is a huge advantage to England particularly in drafting. In Europe, most work in law on a transnational level is done in English. During President Sarkozy's presidency, there was some initial concern about his wish to ensure the EU Commission funded training for judges so they could understand two languages. That concern was shown to be misconceived, as his aim was not to seek greater use of French but to

25 The London Corn Trade Association becoming the Grain and Feed Trade Association (GAFTA) and the Liverpool Cotton Association becoming The International Cotton Association – Cranston page 12.

26 The Time Charterparty standard form first issued by the now defunct New York Produce Exchange in 1913 has offered a choice of law and arbitration venue; its last major revision was in 1993 by ASBA (the Association of Ship Brokers & Agents [US]), BIMCO (the Baltic and International Council) and SMF (the Singapore Maritime Foundation replacing FONASBA (the Federation of National Associations of Ship Brokers & Agents) of New York. ISDA did the same for its standard form.

27 French was the sole language of HCCH until 1964 – see Chapter 2 page <138>.

encourage more French judges to speak English. It was a far cry from the 1980s when during the discussion of the terms of insurance on London market terms for shipping in the event of a NATO war with the Soviet Union, the French delegates relayed instructions said to come from the French President himself that there must be an equally authoritative version in French. The British have also learnt to live with its status as a transnational language. Gone is the concern that when English is used in transnational agreements, it may not be precisely used;[28] there is much less pedantry.

3.1.4 *Law as a Major UK Service industry with the Dominance of Transnational Law Firms*

Until the early 1970s, law firms were largely domestic with offices in UK and a few overseas. The number of partners was limited by statute, so many firms were able to display the names of all their partners on their letterheads. In the period since then the size of the partnerships has expanded exponentially as have their global spread, sometimes through alliances or loose associations or through firms with multiple offices worldwide. Their domestic importance can be seen from the fact that out of total revenue of £47.1bn in 2023, £33.7bn was from the top 100 firms.[29] Their transnational importance can

[28] See Report of the Departmental Advisory Committee on UNCITRAL Model Law [1990] Arb Int 3 (DAC Report on UNCITRAL Arbitration) at page 7.

[29] City UK 2024 Report at pages 6 and 23.

be seen from the fact that law firms that originated in the US and the UK have become the dominant law firms worldwide.[30] Law firms have become major industries in their own right and have, so far, eclipsed accounting firms despite the fact that some of the accounting firms have significant legal departments.[31]

Although the dominant firms originating in the UK and US are regarded as either English or American and their present dominant focus is either UK or US, their practice can be the law of any of the nations in which they have offices and where there are lawyers qualified in that nation. Some assert that they have no ultimate loyalty to the nations in which they originated and could move the balance of their practice to the laws of other nations. It is said therefore they have no ultimate loyalty to any legal system but will shift to the one that is perceived to be in their clients' best interests.

This view cannot be lightly dismissed, particularly now that law is an industry. However, for the present (and many expect for the future) the firms that originated in England or have a major focus on England are anxious to promote the use of English commercial law in transactions

[30] Tables at pages 34–36 of the City UK 2024 Report.

[31] In 2024, PwC had more than 4,000 lawyers operating in over 150 countries, KPMG more than 3,850 lawyers in 84 countries, Deloitte more than 2,400 lawyers in 80 countries, and EY more than 2,400 lawyers in 94 countries. In the UK alone, Deloitte had more than 550 lawyers, putting it close to becoming one of the top 50 law firms in the UK, while PwC had 454 lawyers in the UK, and KPMG had more than 250:. see page 30 of the City UK 2024 Report.

and have a firm loyalty. Philip Wood's *Governing Law Risks in International Business Transactions*[32] provides a carefully argued treatise on the benefits of using English commercial law in comparison to its major competitors.

Moreover, the support given to maintaining English commercial law at the cutting edge remains strong. The Financial Markets Law Committee, established in 2002[33] to identify areas of legal uncertainty or misunderstanding in the London financial markets, receives immense support, primarily in the time spent by leading practitioners in strengthening English commercial law and keeping it in line with change; a glance at its minutes published on its website[34] shows the range of its work. The City of London Law Society and specialist bodies such as the London Shipping Law Centre make similar contributions to maintaining and strengthening the position of English commercial law.

There are also other bodies such as LawTech UK, an enterprise funded by the UK government, which is actively promoting the development of legal technology. One of its offshoots, the UK Jurisdiction Taskforce has produced legal statements answering critical questions as to the operation of English common law in responding to technological changes.

32 (2022) Oxford University Press.

33 In succession to the Financial Law Panel described in Lord Donaldson's Sultan Azlan Shah Lecture.

34 FMLC, *Organisational Structure*, https://fmlc.org/about/organisational-structure/#minutes.

3.1.5 *The Attraction of the UK as a Place for Scholarship, Practice and Study*

The UK is also immensely fortunate in that it is seen as a place of scholarship, for study and for practice by many, particularly the young from different nations; there are over 200 foreign law firms based in the UK from over 40 different jurisdictions.[35] Although the UK faces the stiffest competition from US, the advantages to the UK are immense, for those that come not only stimulate the development of English commercial law, but if they return to their own nations they usually take with them a deep understanding of the quality of English commercial law.

The UK also exports English commercial law in a number of ways. First, others copy and use what England provides free of charge – the so called free rider problem.[36] Second, UK lawyers teach by example the strengths of English commercial law when practising in other nations (whether the systems are similar to England's or not). This is at its most evident in the approach of an English commercial lawyer in negotiating or drafting and in a court or arbitration by command of procedure and skilled advocacy. Third, as English textbooks provide access to English commercial law in a way some of the UK's most distinguished judges have regarded as superior to a code,[37] the free provision of slightly outdated

[35] CityUK Report 2024 at page 26; Lord Bingham pointed out the benefits of this in his 1991 FA Mann Lecture – published in the *Business of Judging*.

[36] As explained in Chapter 2 at page <78>.

[37] Lord Goff as set out in Chapter 2 at page <125>.

editions through a charity, the International Law Book Facility,[38] assists many developing countries in adopting English commercial law.

3.2 What Are the Issues Facing English Commercial Law?

The question that must be asked is why with all these strengths is there any cause for concern about the continued pre-eminence of English commercial law as a national system used for transnational commerce? It is therefore necessary, very briefly, to highlight six issues that reflect the far-reaching and rapid changes in commerce, the different transnational environment and the competition now faced.

3.2.1 *Profound Changes in Commerce and the Development of Transnational Law*

Changes in commerce and the significant effect they are likely to have on law were discussed in Chapter 2. Those were digitalisation; AI and automated decision-making; climate change, environmental concerns and labour standards of employment; compatibility and interoperability; difficulties in resolving choice of law; and the rapid pace of change and its unpredictability. Chapter 2 also traced the development of transnational commercial law from the second half of the nineteenth century through private transnational bodies and the drafting of conventions. This work largely passed in the

[38] ILBF, https://ilbf.org.uk/.

course of the twentieth century to intergovernmental organisations, though the private bodies remain important. The position today is that there are effectively four bodies that produce transnational commercial law: UNIDROIT, UNCITRAL, HCCH (the Hague Conference on Private International Law), and the ICC (International Chamber of Commerce) and other international bodies that produce standard forms.

Although the UK was a major driving force in the private bodies in the nineteenth century, the twentieth century saw a change. Although there was strong participation in the drafting of the Hague Rules 1924, as explained in Chapter 2, some eminent English judges were highly sceptical of the UK government's decision to adopt it. Later that century, the UK stood aside and took its own course on issues such as arbitration (by codifying its own law rather than adopting the UNCITRAL model law)[39] and on international sales by declining to adopt the UN Convention on Contracts for the International Sale of Goods (Vienna, 1980) (CISG).[40] As engagement with this transnational development and other transnational projects is one of the five options put

[39] See DAC Report on UNCITRAL arbitration. The text of the UNCITRAL model law was drafted between 1982 and 1985 when it was approved. The UK participated fully in the discussions.

[40] UNICITRAL, *United Nations Convention on Contracts for the International Sale of Goods*, https://uncitral.un.org/sites/uncitral.un.org/files/media-documents/uncitral/en/19-09951_e_ebook.pdf. One of the features of CISG is that a digest was kept of cases decided under it until 2016. UNICITRAL, *Digest of Case Law on the United Nations Convention on Contracts for the International Sale of Goods*, https://uncitral.un.org/sites/uncitral.un.org/files/media-documents/uncitral/en/cisg_digest_2016.pdf.

forward for further consideration, this subject, with recent developments, is better considered later in the context of that option.

3.2.2 *Change in the Economic Standing of the UK and Shift in International Economic and Trading Dominance*

English commercial law achieved its current status as a result of a number of factors set out in Chapter 2 – (1) political stability, (2) English domination of world trade, (3) the role of the English judiciary and their relationship to the markets, (4) procedure, (5) readiness to consider overseas ideas, (6) a sympathetic executive government, (7) some support from Parliament, (8) some systemisation of the law, and (9) a ready engagement with the development of transnational law, though not as enthusiastic about the outcome in some instances. It is not surprising to conclude that of the three branches of government, it was the judiciary who fostered and developed the characteristics of English commercial law through their relationship with and understanding of the markets that drove the UK economy.

The one critical factor wholly missing today is dominance in world trade. The UK's dominance was one of the, then, mainstays of transnational commerce – trade in goods and commodities, shipping, insurance and banking and finance. It was in these areas that English commercial law developed on the backbone of that dominance that has since passed to other nations. Moreover, other nations, particularly China and the US, are now dominant in the digital industry, in digital commerce and in AI. In comparison with these nations and the EU, the UK is a very much smaller player. The UK is therefore in a materially weaker economic position in competing for digital commerce and digital business and in the use of AI.

3.2.3 *The Executive Government and the Legislature*

In the period in which English commercial law developed transnational status, by and large Parliament and the executive government left the development of commerce and finance to the markets. They relied on the private bodies that provided the governance of the markets through establishing frameworks for dealing, fostering competition (for the most part) and preventing fraud. Self-governance also sought to sustain stability. The power of the Governor of the Bank, the Chairman of the Stock Exchange and the Chairman of Lloyd's were central to this era of self-governance. The occasional intervention of the criminal courts was seen as necessary; the trial at the Old Bailey of Lord Kylsant, a prominent City personage and politician, and John Moreland, a partner of a leading accounting firm, in 1931 was said even as late as the 1970s to have kept the City on its toes. Though there has been a marked change, as there is now extensive regulation particularly in banking and finance by governmental agencies or independent regulators established under legislation (both in the UK and elsewhere), the change in the system from self-governance to a system of state regulation does not appear as yet to have had a significant impact on English commercial law.

Although much is said about the importance of English commercial law, the interest of the executive government depends much on the position taken by individual ministers rather than a focussed government strategy. The severe financial constraint since the 2008 financial crisis has meant that the executive government is an uncertain source of help.[41] The effect of that crisis also had the much less noticed effect of many highly experienced civil servants who had an in-depth command of legal issues being asked to retire to reduce government expenditure; this denuded departments of expertise honed by years of experience. The position has not been helped by responsibility for commercial law being taken by more than one department. Parliament presents the problem that there has always been a general lack of time for legalisation and interest in commercial law. Over the past few years, legislation has generally proceeded by complex and lengthy Bills or through subordinate legislation enabled by ever wider regulatory powers in Bills or by skeleton Bills, which contain nothing but powers to make subordinate legislation.

On the other hand, disinterestedness can have some advantage as commercial law does not become a political football. This may be contrasted with the US where political forces opposed to central bank digital currencies delayed the

[41] It took a very considerable effort to persuade the government in the years preceding 2011 that the premises occupied by the Commercial and TCC Courts in Fetter Lane were wholly unsuitable for international commercial and TCC cases and that the Rolls Building was required; the Rolls Building was opened by Queen Elizabeth II in December 2011.

implementation of the 2022 revisions to Article 12 of the Uniform Commercial Code.

3.2.4 *Competition from Other Systems*

A new factor of some significance is the competition faced by English commercial law manifested in two different respects.

3.2.4.1 Modernisation of the Law of Other Nations

First, other nations are modernising their commercial law. The US with its much larger economy has been since the second half of the twentieth century providing the major competition to English commercial law. It has modernised its Uniform Commercial Code to facilitate the use of new technologies and digital assets.

France revised its Civil Code relating to contractual obligations in 2016. This was the first such major revision since the time of Napoleon over 200 years ago. The revision was accompanied by an excellent English translation, because it was feared that, unless the law of France was brought up to date through a fundamental revision to the Civil Code, the law would fall behind and French lawyers and the French influence across the world (which is fairly profound in a number of countries) would become out of date and in time fall into disuse in transnational transactions. Another example is Germany. About eight years ago the German government first produced a booklet called *Made in Germany*. It explains its purpose:

> 'Made in Germany' is not just a quality seal reserved for German cars or machinery, it is equally applicable to German law. Our laws protect private property and civil liberties, they guarantee harmony and economic success. In the age of economic globalism, law is an important competitive factor. German law forms part of the system of codified law that has evolved throughout continental Europe. It is predictable, affordable.

These three examples illustrate the real consciousness across the world of the need to modernise the law and legal systems so they can properly compete with those of other nations. An aspect of this modernisation has been to adopt more transnational law from the four sources described.

3.2.4.2 Growth in Centres for Dispute Resolution

Second, the success of law firms in both their litigious and non-litigious work has emphasised the economic importance of providing centres for dispute resolution. New York, Geneva, Paris and Stockholm[42] have since the early twentieth century been strong competitors to London as seats for arbitration, but there are many more recent competitors, with Singapore in particular establishing itself as an important

[42] Although England was the first nation to establish institutional international arbitration with the establishment by the City in 1892 of the London Court of International Arbitration, it was followed in the twentieth century by other nations; the ICC Court of Arbitration was established in 1922, the Swedish Chamber of Commerce Committee in 1917, the American Arbitration Association in 1926 and the USSR Arbitration Commission in 1932; see Veeder & Dye page 329.

dispute resolution centre for court, mediation and arbitral resolution of disputes.[43] Other nations have devised new ways of being competitive with France, Germany and the Netherlands enabling commercial cases to be heard in English.[44] I shall return to this.

3.2.5 *Inherent Issues of English Commercial Law*

As foreshadowed in the second chapter, the present century has brought to the fore some of the problems inherent in the way in which English commercial law has developed.

3.2.5.1 Complexity

First, there is the inherent complexity of a system based on case law. Arthur Corbin who taught at Yale from 1903 to 1943 is said[45] to have been the last person who had read all the common law cases on contract law when writing his eight-volume treatise on contract.[46] That has since become an impossible task. Aided though lawyers are by search engines,

[43] The 2025 White & Case International Arbitration Survey carried out with Queen Mary University of London ranked Singapore second after London as the preferred choice for a seat of arbitration. It had ranked equal first with London in the 2022 Survey. see https://www.whitecase.com/insight-our-thinking/2025-international-arbitration-survey.

[44] X. E. Kramer and J. Sorabji (eds.) (2019) *International Business Courts*, 11th International Publishing, Open Access, https://boeken.rechtsgebieden.boomportaal.nl/publicaties/9789462369719?q=business+courts&BoomToken=JrMB5g%2bH16jNYfNPeqPxuQ#9.

[45] By Professor Grant Gilmore.

[46] A Comprehensive Treatise on the Working Rules of Contracts Law.

the mass of material makes ascertaining the law on particular points difficult and costly, unless authoritative textbooks are available.

3.2.5.2 Diminished Opportunity for Development

Second, although as just pointed out there are substantial disadvantages to a system that has a vast case law and therefore a dearth of cases before the courts might seem an advantage, a system that depends for its development on case law needs cases to keep it up to date. As Dame Hazel Genn has pointed out,[47] there has been a major shift from public dispute resolution to private dispute resolution. In financial services the success of the financial ombudsman scheme has removed from the courts all cases within its purview including those involving SMEs, which were often a fruitful source of law for commercial cases;[48] it has at the same time created its own body of case law with its own special status. As I pointed out, somewhat controversially in 2016, the effect of the reform to the Arbitration Act had been to reduce the types and number of cases coming to the courts on points of

[47] In her 2012 F. A. Mann Lecture, *Why the Privatisation of Civil Justice Is a Rule of Law Issue*, www.ucl.ac.uk/laws/sites/laws/files/36th-f-a-mann-lecture-19.11.12-professor-hazel-genn.pdf.

[48] See Lord Thomas, *The Common Law in Private Dispute Resolution's Shadow*, lecture on 9 July 2018 at the Max Planck Institute for Comparative and International Private Law, Hamburg, on the occasion of its annual Sommerkonzil, Rabels Zeitschrift für ausländisches und internationales Privatrecht, vol. 83 (RabelsZ 83), 487–506.

law arising in an arbitration;[49] but there may be other ways to make clear the rich sources of English commercial law, such as systematic publication of arbitration awards and the decisions of other non-court bodies that make decisions on legal issues.[50]

3.3 What Are the Options for Enabling English Commercial Law to Maintain Its Position?

If some or all of the matters just described are accepted as needing consideration, what then are the prospects for the future development of English commercial law? It is neither practicable nor sensible to offer predictions – there are now too many uncertainties. However, it is practicable to outline some options that need to be considered if English commercial law is to maintain its position as the dominant national system for transnational commercial law and not see itself overtaken by other national systems or by the development of transnational law.

[49] 2016 BAILII Lecture, 9 March 2016, www.bailii.org/bailii/lecture/04.pdf. For the controversy engendered and a contrary view, see, for example, Dame Elizabeth Gloster, *Symbiosis or Sadomasochism? The relationship between the courts and arbitration* (2018) 34(3) Arbitration International 321 at 332.

[50] See Lord Thomas, *The Common Law in Private Dispute Resolution's Shadow*; see also Sir Bernard Rix, 12 March 2015 Jones Day Professorship in Commercial Law Lecture, SMU, Singapore 12 March 2015.

It is, however, important to bear in mind, the views expressed at the turn of the nineteenth and twentieth centuries by Mr T. G. Carver QC, the author of one of the leading textbooks on Carriage of Goods by Sea. When speaking of the need for transnational agreement on issues relating to marine insurance in 1899, he argued that agreement on the principles relating to constructive total loss in marine insurance was of importance to the progress of transnational commerce.[51] None was ever reached and it has made no difference. Will a similar view be expressed sometime in the future about some of the matters highlighted? Could it be then said that the UK managed perfectly well by just muddling on, as the people of the UK have done with the Union that is the UK as discussed in Chapter 1?

The options considered here are:

1. Promoting English commercial law more vigorously but otherwise leaving well alone.
2. Taking more active steps to facilitate and strengthen the development of English case law as up to date and internationalist in outlook.
3. Promoting codification and restatements.
4. Strengthening engagement in the development of transnational law.
5. Pursuing leadership of the gradualist role of commercial courts in developing law that is used transnationally.

In each of these, I want to look at the option of going alone or seeking to promote transnational law or taking the course of

[51] See Chapter 2 at page <131>.

something in the middle. In 1997, Sir Roy Goode expressed the need for the UK to be more outward looking and observed on return to the UK, although uplifted as regards the judiciary, he was depressed by 'the state of our statute book and by our inertia and complacent belief in the innate superiority of English commercial law'.[52]

3.3.1 *Option 1: Promoting English Commercial Law More Vigorously but Otherwise Leaving Well Alone*

Some might take the view that all is well and there is no need to worry – all that needs to be done is to promote the strengths of English commercial law. The work being done by LegalUK is outstanding[53] and, subject to being provided with better financial resources, it is difficult to see how it could be done better. This is an option, but it must be viewed against the various factors I have set out and the other options.

3.3.2 *Option 2: Taking More Active Steps to Facilitate and Strengthen the Development of English Case Law as up to Date and Internationalist in Outlook*

Chapter 2 examined the pre-eminent role of the judges in developing commercial law by case law in England at the time of the UK's domination of transnational commerce. That role

[52] Goode Hamlyn Lectures page 100.

[53] LegalUK, https://legaluk.org.

has been the foundation of the success of English commercial law in obtaining its widely used transnational status. That continued success can be seen in Fintech.[54] But it is necessary to dig more deeply.

3.3.2.1 A Change in the Civilian (Civil Law) Nations

First a word about competition. The English common law method of developing commercial law through case law has been seen as one of England's unique characteristics. It is sometimes asserted that development by case law is anathema to the civilian tradition, that tradition has to rely on legislatures enacting legislation that will never have the agility to keep the law up to date in comparison with a case law system. That may be a traditional view, but it is easy to forget the developments that have been made by the Strasbourg and Luxembourg Courts who have developed public law (sometimes criticised as judicial activism) through case law. In the sphere of private law or 'lawyer's law' (where, just as in the UK, there is little concern about judicial activism) the importance of precedent in developing civil law in civilian jurisdictions is not receiving sufficient attention in the UK. As has been demonstrated by a leading European scholar, Professor Christina Ramberg,[55] other nations now see the demonstrable

[54] See, for example, cases cited by Lord Hodge (October 2022) *The Rule of Law, the Courts and the British Economy* [2023] LMCLQ 34 at page 46.

[55] 4th Ole Lando Memorial Lecture at the European Law Institute, Madrid Conference (2022), Professor Christina Ramberg, *The Interaction between Soft Law and Case Law: How Precedents Fulfil Ole Lando's Ambitions to Harmonize European Contract Law* (2023) 31(1) European

benefits of developing their law through the decisions of judges in cases so that their law is not only certain and predictable but also flexible and quickly adaptable. Some nations have added refinements to the way a case law system works; for example, in about ten cases a year, the French Cour de Cassation issues opinions without waiting for cases to come from the lower courts; two nations with two major economies, China and Brazil, have authorised their Supreme Courts to provide binding summaries of principles to be derived from their cases.

As others see the merits of the way in which English commercial law is developed, it is more important to follow the example of the great eighteenth-and nineteenth-century judges, as explained in Chapter 2, in two main ways. First, by ensuring the judges are kept in close touch with markets and scientific developments and, secondly, by looking to other systems of law.

3.3.2.2 Keeping in Close Touch with Commerce and Science

The UK is extremely fortunate in the different ways in which the judges are kept in close touch with commerce and science. If judges are to make decisions that are in line with commercial practice and scientific development and to demonstrate that they do in fact understand the expectations of business, it is not possible at a time of such profound, rapid and unpredictable change to rely on what

Review of Private Law 3. She gave examples from Brazil, China, France and Sweden.

they may have learnt in practice even a few years earlier or from occasional discussions or from what they are told by advocates in court. That may have been possible for Scrutton LJ,[56] whose family was so heavily involved in shipping and commerce, but it is not possible today. The mistaken decision of the House of Lords[57] in holding unlawful interest rate swaps made by local authorities in good faith and for a proper commercial purpose is a good example, as Lord Bingham pointed out,[58] of showing how important it is to understand the market.

Beginning about twelve years ago, first in relation to criminal law, particularly the science of the mind and forensic science, the Royal Society has played a much needed role in ensuring that the major developments in science are discussed with judges and the best scientific guidance is given to the courts.[59] The Royal Society has a world-leading role in this and is now working with the US National Academy of

[56] See the illuminating discussion in Foxton Life of Scrutton at pages 267–273 where the author examines the difficulty of ensuring 'commercial situation sense'.

[57] *Hazell v Hammersmith and Fulham LBC* [1992] 2 A.C. 1 (Lord Templeman giving the main judgment), reversing the decision of a Divisional Court presided over by Woolf LJ and a Court of Appeal containing Bingham LJ and Nicholls LJ [1990] 2 Q.B. 697.

[58] *The Law as the Handmaid of Commerce* (2001), 16th Sultan Azlan Shah Lecture published in Lord Bingham (2011) *Lives of the Law*, Oxford University Press at page 283 and www.sultanazlanshah.com/pdf/2004%20Book%201/SAS_Lecture_16.pdf.

[59] One example is the production of primers on subjects such as statistics and DNA; see https://royalsociety.org/about-us/what-we-do/science-and-law/.

Sciences.[60] Similarly, the Financial Markets Law Committee has for some years provided an annual seminar on changing practices in the financial markets and occasional seminars for the judges of the Financial List. There is a need to ensure that these examples are coordinated and replicated across the UK's courts.

3.3.2.3 Looking Overseas

There are many reasons for looking at how other nations resolve issues of commercial law. If a court is laying down principles that are likely to be followed transnationally, it is necessary to take account of the available views, both legal and market, of other jurisdictions, not only to have the benefit of those views but also to show that English courts respect the views of others in relation to their law and to their markets, which are increasingly dominant.[61] If English commercial law is to continue as a system used transnationally, then it must demonstrate it is transnational in the way it makes law.

[60] In the October 2023 Conference, *Science in the Interests of Justice*, wider areas were considered including likelihood ratios, digital evidence, the science of climate change and generative AI. The report of the conference is at: https://royalsociety.org/-/media/about-us/what-we-do/science-in-the-interest-of-justice-conference-report.pdf.

[61] As Lord Bingham pointed out in his 1991 F. A. Mann Lecture published in *The Business of Judging* at page 99, the receptiveness of English law to overseas influence was (1) the engagement of commercial practitioners in London in disputes on foreign law in learning that English law was not the sole repository of wisdom and (2) the settling of foreign scholars in London particularly Germans such as Dr Frances Mann and the work of the comparativists.

English courts have always done this, as explained in Chapter 2 and as summarised by Lord Bingham:[62]

> Home-grown solutions and rules, however serviceable in their own day, may no longer serve. A broader transnational approach, drawing on the experience and wisdom of businessmen and lawyers all round the world, is called for. Mansfield's close attention to the laws and customs of foreign countries points the way.

Forging a common transnational approach[63] can also mitigate the effect of the UK's decision not to adopt conventions or model laws establishing transnational laws. The UK's

[62] see Chapter 2 pages 101–102 and Lord Bingham in his Sultan Azlan Shah Lecture at page 284. In his 2005 Maccabean Lecture, Lord Bingham said at page 69:

> A national judge seeking to rely on a foreign law is well advised to proceed with great caution, since many pitfalls await the unlearned, the unguided and the superficial. It would be naïve to suppose that a better answer to difficult legal problems is always to be found elsewhere. That said, however, there is, as I would suggest, a real gain, even if only in a very small minority of cases, in drawing on the learning of other jurists grappling with very much the same problems in other jurisdictions. We cannot claim a monopoly of learning and wisdom. But to draw inspiration from the wisdom of others involves a conscious voyage beyond the bounds of the inherited common law.

[63] The decision of the Privy Council in *Betamax v State Corporation* [2021] UK PC 14, an appeal from Mauritius provided an opportunity to show that the provisions of the UNCITRAL model law on arbitration and the English Arbitration Act had an identical approach to challenging an award on the grounds of public policy, though demonstrating this was made easier by the UK's long-standing accession to the 1958 New York Convention on the enforcement of arbitral awards where the provisions on public policy are very similar to those of the UNCIYTAL Model law.

departure from the EU has diminished the UK's ability to influence the development of the harmonised law of one of the three of the world's most important trading blocs whilst it might also curtail the influence of civilian law on English commercial law. Some see this as an advantage as it enables the common law to re-assert its bright line difference; others see the lessening of the influence is isolating English commercial law from broader development.

Good faith provides an illustration of how this might be approached. Lord Mansfield introduced into English law the concept of good faith and, if he had not had an extraordinarily conservative successor, that may have become a concept enshrined in English law as a general part of the law of obligations and not confined, as it has become, to the law of insurance and reinsurance. It was therefore very encouraging to see the concept revisited by Leggatt J in the Commercial Court in 2013[64] where he described English law as running against the tide even in other common law jurisdictions. Much has been said about this in other cases and by scholars,[65] but it was vital that this development be viewed

[64] *Yam Seng Pte Ltd v International Trade* Corporation [2013] EWHC 111 (QB) at paragraphs 119–154.

[65] Goode Hamlyn Lectures at pages 19–20; Ewan McKendrick (2021) *Contract Law*, 14th edition, Red Globe, ch. 12.10.3–4; Magda Raczynska and Paul S. Davies (eds.) (2020) *Contents of Commercial Contracts Affecting Freedoms*, Hart, chapter 5, Good Faith and Contract Terms, and chapter 6, Excluding Good Faith and Restricting Discretion; Hector MacQueen, *European Contract Law in the Post-Brexit and (Post?)-Pandemic United Kingdom*, 3rd Ole Lando Memorial lecture [2022] European Review of Private law 3.

from the perspective of the markets. If it was not viewed from this perspective, English commercial law would be departing from one of its fundamental characteristics and strengths. Such a view was provided by the FMLC in November 2022 in a published paper[66] where attention was particularly drawn to the risks of undermining contractual certainty and to the difficulties of adding a general principle found in continental codes without fundamentally reappraising and rewriting English contract law.

Essential though it is for English courts to remain abreast of developments worldwide, it is not easy to ensure this. The courts depend to a considerable extent on the lawyers for the parties assisting the courts with the provision of materials of this kind. Generally, the parties do not view with any real enthusiasm the court conducting its own research without reference to them. Just as the view is often taken in arbitrations that the parties are interested in having their dispute decided and not paying for the development of the law (save where a market wants a wide-ranging decision for the benefit of the market), there is quite naturally a decline in the appetite to fund the wider provision of materials. It is unfortunate that the executive government has abandoned the position that one of the reasons for keeping court fees low was to acknowledge the role of the litigants in developing the law. HM Treasury has from the time of Bentham and throughout the nineteenth century and twentieth centuries

[66] FMLC, *Duties of Good Faith in the Financial Markets*, https://fmlc.org/wp-content/uploads/2022/12/FMLC-Paper-Duties-of-Good-Faith-in-Wholesale-Financial-Contracts.pdf.

gradually, but successfully, transferred to litigants the cost of providing courts to decide civil disputes. Although challenged by powerful lawyer Lord Chancellors (when the UK had such), HM Treasury has resisted the argument that the state should bear some of the cost because of wider public benefit of developing the law.[67] Given current and foreseeable fiscal circumstances, it is unlikely that this position will change.

The question therefore has to be addressed as to how, particularly in the light of the fact that the amount of material available constantly grows, better and better coordinated assistance is to be achieved. I shall return to this in my conclusion.

3.3.3 *Option 3: Promoting Codification and Restatements*

I can take together codification by Parliament and restatements of the law as the third option.

3.3.3.1 Codification

There were in the nineteenth century, as discussed in Chapter 2,[68] campaigns for codification that resulted in partial codifications from 1882 to 1906 in then important areas of the law – sale of goods, finance through negotiable instruments and insurance. Is codification relevant today?

[67] Lord Thomas, *The Maintenance of Local Justice*, 2004 Sir Elwyn Jones Memorial Lecture, Bangor University, 3 Welsh Legal History Society 182 at pages 219–220.

[68] See Chapter 2 pages <117–124>.

The advantages of codification[69] include: (1) making the law simpler, clearer and more accessible; (2) making it is easier to find the answer to legal problems; (3) modernising and updating law; (4) avoiding the need to wait and see if a point of law on which the law is uncertain comes up for decision; (5) resolving uncertainty either because of a lack of precedent or the existence of conflicting precedents; (6) distilling the vast amount of case law; and (7) overcoming the restrictions in the common law in its ability to develop the law by the need to respect precedent and by judicial restraint on the scope of judicial legislation. Furthermore (8), consistent with the aim of increasing the use of English commercial law, making it easier to 'export', expanding its influence and strengthening its economic advantages.[70]

The major arguments against codification are rigidity (or the loss of flexibility) and obsolescence – the freezing of the law as it was at the stage it had been developed when it was codified. There is also the risk of the courts interpreting such a statute in accordance with established principles, which might result in decisions that would not have been reached had the courts had a greater flexibility to state what the law should be. There is the further difficulty that if a code is wrongly interpreted or becomes out of date, then there are real difficulties in amending the codified law. An eminent

[69] As summarised by Lady Arden in her Combar Lecture at 203–205; by Halston at 161–166; and by Sir Roy Goode, *The Codification of Commercial Law* (1988) 14 Monash UL Rev 135 (Sir Wilfred Fullagar Memorial Lecture 1988) (Goode Fullagar) at 137–140.

[70] Halston at 163–165.

view has been expressed[71] that reform of the common law by statute should be restricted to areas where the law is based on statute or a wrong decision has been taken and there is no time to await the decision of the highest court to put it right.

However, whatever the merits of these arguments, there are two impediments. First, there is often considerable judicial scepticism about the benefits of codification. As Lord Goff observed in respect of a code that simply restates the law:[72]

> The code is like a photograph: it records the law as it has developed at a particular point in time. Moreover, it is not possible for any code to provide an absolutely accurate, still less a complete statement of the law on any topic. The camera will, as usual, lie . . .. Let codification be the work of jurists rather than legislators.

Second, and more importantly, the reality is that getting Parliament to enact codified commercial law is a formidable, if not an almost impossible, task. Leaving aside the experience of the Victorian age, the Law Commission's project on codification of contract law, though greeted by great enthusiasm,[73] failed. The Law Commission had attempted, as part of its first programme after its creation in 1965, to produce a contract code in conjunction with the Scottish Law Commission. Harvey McGregor QC was engaged to produce a draft that

[71] Lord Andrew Burrows: *Legislative Reform of Remedies for Breach of Contract*: The English Perspective [1977] Edinburgh Law Review 155; Halston at 167–172.

[72] See Goff Maccabean Lecture at 172.

[73] Halston at 151; and Goode Fullagar at 136.

reformed the law rather than restating it; there were fundamental differences of opinion between the Scottish law Commissions and the England and Wales Law Commission, which resulted in the Scottish Law Commission withdrawing in 1971. Work was suspended in 1972. The decision was made to adopt a topic-by-topic approach in areas such as exemption clauses and the supply of goods in bulk, which resulted in some statutory reform[74] but with little support from the executive government or Parliament.[75]

In 1993 a scathing view was expressed by a preeminent commercial arbitrator, V. V. Veeder QC[76] at the failure to enact a code for arbitration law:

> That the government should appear so indifferent is perhaps surprising. Amongst trading nations, the United Kingdom is uniquely dependent upon international trade and upon the decisions of international traders, bankers, insurers and others to do business in London or by

[74] Arden Combar Lecture.

[75] An example was the failure to take forward the widely supported recommendations on the reform of non-disclosure and breach of warranty in Law Commission Report (1980) *Non-disclosure and Breach of warranty* (Report 104); as a result of the 1906 Act and court decisions, the law had become unfair and only mitigated as regards the consumer by undertakings given by the Association of British Insurers not to rely on the strict application of the law. The reform to the Bills of Lading Act 1855 recommended by the Law Commission Report (1991) on *Rights of Suit on Carriage of Goods by Sea* (Report 196) was enacted, despite the government making no parliamentary time for its debate in the Commons, by the good fortune that no time was needed as there was no opposition to the bill.

[76] Veeder & Dye at page 350. For the nineteenth attempt see Chapter 2 page 123.

> reference to English commercial law and practise.
> If English commercial law is popular with the international community it is not because England is a great financial power or because a vast domestic market supports the English legal system, as in the USA Germany and Japan. It is perhaps because English commercial law has two attributes not equally shared by many other legal systems: certainty in establishing what the legal answer is to any given situation and the predictability as to what the answer would be to that situation by an English court or arbitration tribunal. Both are jeopardised when the government fails to implement essential law reform.

Then came the Arbitration Act 1996 and its undoubted great success. The law before that Act could only be ascertained by reference to textbooks[77]and there was no easy method of distilling, particularly for foreign lawyers or lay litigants so important to arbitration in England, the well-developed principles contained in the cases. The achievement of the 1996 Act was due to the Departmental Advisory Committee on Arbitration under the successive chairmanships of Lord Mustill, Lord Steyn and Lord Saville.[78] It was in part codification, in part reform and in part leaving to one side difficult

[77] Russell (first published in 1889), Hogg (1936) and Mustill & Boyd (1982).

[78] With a carefully thought through means of drafting the bill (Lord Steyn, *England's Response to the Model Law of Arbitration* [1994] [Lord Steyn BILA lecture] at pages 8–9, https://bila.org.uk/wp-content/uploads/old/4ff4163fa15112.36610016.pdf) and brilliant younger people to help them such as the late V. V. Veeder QC, Toby Landau KC and Roger Fayers at the DTI (see Lord Mustill's note in 2014 [2016] 16 Arb Int 313–314).

issues such as confidentiality and in part influenced by the UNCITRAL Model Law.

However, since then, despite the enactment of some reforms[79] and the approval by the House of Lords in 2010 for 'uncontroversial' bills to be subject to a procedure under which the Committee stage is undertaken in a Special Public Bill Committee within a period of forty working days, there are no real grounds for thinking that codification has any realistic prospects in Parliament.

The Welsh government and Senedd have taken a different view on codification, as explained in Chapter 1;[80] however. Wales' scope for law-making in private law is extremely limited and its example in engaging with the Law Commission in codification, as outlined earlier, does not yet appear to be one that is attractive to Parliament or the executive government in London.

3.3.3.2 Restatements

Although the drafting and enactment of the Uniform Commercial Code during the 1940s and 1950s in each of the fifty states of the United States was an achievement that no other common law nation has really emulated, it has not

[79] Such as (1) Law Commission Report 242, *Privity of Contract: Contracts for the benefit of Third Parties* leading to the Contracts (Rights of Third Parties) Act 1999; (2) the acceptance of the need to reform the law of insurance as raised in the 1980 Report leading to the Consumer Insurance (Disclosure and Representations) Act 2012 and the Insurance Act 2015; (3) the updating of the Arbitration Act 1996 recommended by the Law Commission in its 2023 Report reviewing the 1996 Act, which was enacted with some amendments in the Arbitration Act 2025.

[80] See Chapter 1 page <34>.

overcome the problems of obsolescence.[81] It was concerns in relation to obsolescence and rigidity that has led the US into a different solution in other areas of the law – setting out the principles in various fields of law that could be derived from cases across the several states in that field by what was described as a 'restatement of the law'. The idea for this can be traced back to the US Supreme Court Justice Joseph Story in the early nineteenth century who foresaw the problems and suggested a code for Massachusetts to be interpreted as a code of the common law and not as a statute.[82] His views were considered over the following century and led in 1923 to the founding of the American Law Institute. The writing of restatements has been the principal work of the American Law Institute. It published its first restatements between 1932 and 1937.[83] This method and the constant revisions to restatements that are required can be seen as having served the US well.

Restating the law has been emulated in the UK by Lord Burrows[84] assisted by a small team. Work is underway

[81] Robert E. Scott (2023) The Uniform Commercial Code and the Ongoing Quest for an Efficient and Fair Commercial law. In The American Law Institute, *A Centennial History* (ed. Gold and Gordon), Oxford University Press at page 273 (ALI Centennial History).

[82] David J. Seipp (2023) The Need for Restatement of the Common Law: A Long Look Back, published in ALI Centennial History.

[83] Kenneth S. Abraham and G. Edward White (2023) The Work of the American Law Institute in Its Historical Context, published in ALI Centennial History.

[84] Lord Burrows (2013) *Restatement of the Law of Unjust Enrichment*, Oxford University Press; and Lord Burrows (2020) *Restatement of the English Law of Contract*, Oxford University Press, 2nd edition.

by a group to provide a similar restatement of English Commercial Law.[85] A restatement has significant advantages. It is not a code but states the law in principles with reference to the cases from which it is derived. It is in no way binding on courts. Its statements of the principles can be revised, kept up to date and modified as cases develop the law. However, it is difficult to see how restatements could be formulated and command the wide acceptance that restatements have commanded in the US without some institutional structure, market input and support. This is another matter to which I will return in my conclusion.

3.3.4 *Option 4: Strengthening UK Engagement in the Development of Transnational Law*

The development of transnational law through international bodies, first private and then state, has a 150-year history outlined in Chapter 2.[86] There was enthusiasm from the UK, which appears to have been grounded in the expectation that others would base transnational law on the principles of English commercial law, but this was not perceived by some leading English judges at the time to have been the result achieved in one of the most important conventions – the Hague Rules.

[85] Gerard McMeel KC, *A Code of English Commercial Law* [2021] LMCLQ 181. It has also been suggested by Lord David Anderson of Ipswich KC, in his 2023 Renton Lecture [2004] P.L.604, that the time had come for there to be a restatement of the UK's constitutional arrangements, based on the work of the American Law Institute.

[86] See Chapter 2 pages <126–139>.

There is currently great activity generally in the development of transnational law, with strong international support and market interest. This has not always been the case as is clear from the failed attempts in 1978 and in 2008 to revise conventions relating to carriage of goods by sea.[87] The interest in transnational law is bolstered by the view that it will provide a fairer system for trade and commerce than the existing systems and enable those in commerce to access law more easily and fairly, particularly given the cost for SMEs of using lawyers.[88] There was also on the creation of UNCTAD and UNCITRAL a view of the developing nations that major change was needed;[89] this was evident in the UNCTAD Report on marine insurance[90] and in the desire to shift the balance in carriage of goods by sea in favour of cargo interests through the Hamburg Rules, 1978. Of longer-term

[87] The failure of the UNCITRAL Hamburg Rules 1978 (UN Convention on Carriage of Goods by Sea) which was ratified by thirty-one states but by no major trading nation and of the subsequent attempt in the UNCITRAL Rotterdam Rules 2008, which was ratified by five states; see Franics Reynolds (2020) Do Carriers Require Special Treatment? In *The World of Maritime and Commercial Law, Essays in Honour of Francis Rose* (ed. C. Mitchell and S. Watterson), Hart.

[88] See Professor Hugh Beale, First Ole Lando Memorial Lecture, *Transnational Contract Law: Lando's Contribution and the Way Forward* (Beale) [2020] European Review of Private Law pages 465–486 at paragraphs 14–16.

[89] As explained in Martin Daunton (2023) *The Economic Government of the World 1933–2023*, Penguin, at page 415 et seq.

[90] UNCTAD Marine Insurance. TD/B/C.4/ISL/27 20 November 1978, paragraph 45; repeated in the 1982 revision of the report, https://unctad.org/system/files/official-document/c4isl27rev1_en.pdf. See Chapter 2 at pages <135–136>.

importance has been nationalism; relying on model laws and conventions is attractive, as it enables nations to embrace a transnational system of law without making recourse to the national system of another nation.

A feature of the current approach is to proceed more by way of model laws than by way of international conventions, as getting a convention agreed or amended is so difficult.[91] Model laws do not take effect as uniform laws under international agreements but are model provisions of law each state can use to make its own law conform to a uniform international standard. This can be seen as a means of harmonisation. Experience seems to suggest that it is easier to get nations to agree when they have the greater freedom that a model law allows in adapting their national system to operate transnationally, as is shown by the significant take up of the instruments drafted by UNCITRAL, UNIDROIT and other bodies.

3.3.4.1 UNCITRAL

The work of UNCITRAL, the intergovernmental body established in the 1960s, has been significant, but the UK's attitude has been ambivalent. As mentioned, the UK did not adopt

[91] As, for example, the failed attempts to revise CISG – see Beale at paragraphs 48–49 and the more recent experience discussed in *Developing Uniform Laws in Private and Commercial Law: Some Lessons Learned, and a Look Ahead*, the 5th Ole Lando Memorial Lecture on 6 September 2023 by the Deputy Secretary-General of UNIDROIT, Professor Anna Veneziano (not yet published but only available as a summary), https://europeanlawinstitute.eu/news-events/news-contd/news/2023-eli-annual-conference-fifth-ole-lando-memorial-lecture-by-prof-veneziano/.

CISG[92] (now adopted by 97 nations)[93] or the Model Law on Arbitration (now adopted by 93 nations).[94] In respect of arbitration where England adopted its own code in 1996, it is important to recall that the pre-eminent practitioner and judge in relation to arbitration, Lord Mustill, was part of the UK delegation that attended the drafting meetings of UNCITRAL.[95] It was again Lord Mustill who chaired the Departmental Committee on Arbitration charged with considering its adoption in England and conducting the consultation.[96] In recommending against adoption[97] in its 1989 report, Lord Mustill's committee gave cogent and powerful reasons: a model law was not a convention; the model law on arbitration was not a complete code; it was not drafted in

92 It maintains a data base on cases decided on all UNCITRAL texts – CLOUT, www.uncitral.org/clout/index.jspx.

93 Including the US, Japan, Germany, France, Australia, Canada and New Zealand. The UK Department of Trade and Industry consulted in 1989: *United Nations Convention on Contracts for the International Sale of Goods: A Consultative Document.* In 1997, Lord Steyn urged the UK's adoption of CISG in his lecture: *The Role of Good Faith and Fair Dealing in Contract Law: A Hair-Shirt Philosophy?* (1991) 6 Denning LJ 131 at 135 and in 1993; Sir Roy Goode also did so: *Insularity or Leadership? The Role of the UK in the Harmonisation of Commercial Law* published in Goode (2018) *The Development of Transnational Commercial Law*, Oxford University Press at page 83.

94 But not in New York, Sweden, Switzerland or France.

95 Lord Wilberforce represented the Chartered Institute of Arbitrators. Martin Hunter, a leading arbitration practitioner at Freshfields and Essex Court Chambers represented the International Bar Association.

96 1987 printed in [1989] Arb Int 278.

97 See DAC Report on UNCITRAL Arbitration and see also Chapter 2 at page <139>.

terms of a UK statute; England had a developed law and enacting a new law would mean starting all over again with learning the new law, whereas in nations with a law that was not so developed the model law would have great advantages.[98] Speaking in the mid-1990s, Lord Steyn[99] contrasted the decision not to enact the model law on arbitration with England's decision not to enact the CISG:

> Cynical foreign observers say that the decision [in respect of the UNCITRAL model law on Arbitration] is in character with England's role in the process of harmonization of international trade law. Typically, they say, England is voluble at international congresses in promoting common law solutions in the framing of a convention and, having achieved significant success in that pursuit, England then rejects the convention as being inferior to native English law. This criticism is obviously too extravagant in its scope. But it is not entirely groundless. The Vienna Sales Convention has been ratified by 34 nations, including almost all the member countries of the European Economic Community, and most of the major trading nations of the world. My understanding is that Belgium, Japan, and New Zealand will also ratify. Yet England delays. I believe the reason is to be found in the deep-seated antipathy of English lawyers towards multilateral conventions. The purity of the common law prevails

[98] See DAC Report on UNCITRAL Arbitration at page 14: 'That this is a serious detriment to be weighed against the potential benefits of enacting the Model Law emerged clearly from the discussion within the Working Group.'

[99] Lord Steyn BILA lecture.

> over the needs of international commerce, and our own trading position. Moreover, as Professor Barry Nicholas, a United Kingdom delegate at the Vienna working sessions, pointed out earlier this year, it is vital that the United Kingdom should ratify the convention quickly, so that the experience of English lawyers and of the Commercial Court can influence the way in which the convention is interpreted and applied. I would argue, however, that the decision of the DAC to recommend that England should not adopt the Model Law was justified on special grounds. And it is right to point out that the committee took this decision under the chairmanship of Lord Justice Mustill and after a most detailed and rigorous examination of the merits and demerits of the Model Law as compared with English law.

As Lord Mustill's successor as chair, Lord Steyn accepted that, although some of the arguments by the 1990s were not as strong as they had been a few years earlier, the decision had been right, as English commercial law had achieved the right balance between party autonomy and judicial scrutiny. Scotland took a different view and adopted the model law.[100]

Some thirty years on, digital commerce has provided a new opportunity to consider the UK's approach to model laws. It is probably impracticable for traders, shipowners and banks worldwide to change from the use of paper trade documents such as bills of lading and bills of exchange to the use of digitalised trade documents without legal principles

[100] See Chapter 2 note 84.

that ensure transnational compatibility and acceptability. In 2017 UNCITRAL produced a Model Law on Electronic Records (MLETR) in an attempt to provide such a transnational system of law. Because of the importance of possession of a set of paper bills of lading as developed historically in most national systems (as derived from the practice of traders as developed and fine-tuned by English commercial law), it was necessary to address the issue of possession. The Model Law dealt with this by providing that control of a digital bill of lading was to be the equivalent of possession.[101]

In 2021 Singapore amended its legislation to adopt MLETR very much in the form in which the MLETR was drafted; in particular, the MLETR concept of control was adopted as the equivalent of possession. The UK has followed a different approach. Although it has followed the MLETR generally in respect of all requirements other than possession, the Electronic Trade Documents Act 2023 has retained the concept of possession; it simply stated that an electronic bill

[101] Article 11 provided:

1. Where the law requires or permits the possession of a transferable document or instrument, that requirement is met with respect to an electronic transferable record if a reliable method is used: *(a)* To establish exclusive control of that electronic transferable record by a person; and *(b)* To identify that person as the person in control.
2. Where the law requires or permits transfer of possession of a transferable document or instrument, that requirement is met with respect to an electronic transferable record through the transfer of control over the electronic transferable record.

of lading can be possessed if there is exclusive control. It was intended that the very well-developed scheme of English case law could be maintained in this way and the flexibility of English commercial law retained for future development. A short Act adapted UK law (as it applies in Scotland and Northern Ireland too) in line with the UNCITRAL model law. The French government sent representatives to the UK to examine how it should implement MLETR; the representatives recommended changes to the French Civil Code[102] strongly influenced by the UK approach. France made the changes to its law on 5 June 2024 so that electronic documents have been given the same legal status as their paper equivalents.

As English commercial law is chosen as the law for many bills of lading used in transnational commerce, it is important, if English commercial law is to maintain that position, that it is and, more importantly, that it is seen to be, entirely interoperable with laws that are based entirely on the MLETR and is interpreted in that way by the UK courts.[103] As was clear from the evidence of expert lawyers

[102] The French Committee of the ICC and Europlace published a white paper in September 2022 urging the benefits of digitalisation, www.icc-france.fr/wp-content/uploads/2022/09/ICC_France_WhitePaper_.pdf; report to the French government detailing changes needed was made in July 2023, www.diplomatie.gouv.fr/IMG/pdf/rapporttrade-_vf-29.06.23_cle08ea4a.pdf.

[103] Although the Bill was not drafted to make that clear (and could not easily be amended to put that on the face of the Bill), the Minister was careful to make that clear in Parliament; see Hansard 20 February 2023, vol. 827 col. 7.

and judges given in January 2023 to the Special Public Bill Committee of the House of Lords,[104] a short but clearly drafted statutory change to English commercial law is intended to make it interoperable. The essential characteristics of English commercial law in upholding freedom of contract, certainty and predictability have been met, it is hoped, in this way, as have the needs of the market in the digital age by provisions that do not depend on any specific technology and allow for the inevitably unpredictable technological development.

In adapting English commercial law, great technical expertise and practical experience is required. Practitioner input and the involvement of the markets are central. The discussions in relation to the 2018 UNCITRAL Model Law on the Recognition of and Enforcement of Insolvency-related judgments and its impact on the Rule in *Gibbs*[105] shows how vital it is for change to be carefully considered by those with a detailed understanding of law and commercial practice.[106]

[104] In accordance with the procedure for Law Commission bills. The written and oral evidence is at https://committees.parliament.uk/committee/636/electronic-trade-documents-bill-hl-special-public-bill-committee/publications/.

[105] *Gibbs* v *S.A. Industriele et Commericiale des Metaux* (1890) 25 Q.B.D. 399.

[106] The Insolvency Service organises 'Forward Thinking Conferences' at which such issues are discussed. The rule in *Gibbs* was discussed in its conference on 10 November 2023, https://sites.google.com/view/forward-thinking-2023/home.

3.3.4.2 UNIDROIT and HCCH

The work of UNIDROIT provides four important examples of the growth of transnational law, but again the attitude of the UK has been ambivalent.

The first example is an instrument in which governments did not participate but that has had widespread influence as soft law – the *UNIDROIT Principles of International Commercial Contracts* (UPICC) first published in 1994. It is now in its fourth version.[107] Each of the working groups that produced the versions have had strong UK representation.[108] The objective, realised in the result, was to produce transnational principles that commanded a consensus[109] and that would lead to the best results in most situations rather than being based on the lowest common denominator between legal systems. The principles largely are a restatement but contain provisions that develop the law. They have had some influence on courts, including the UK Supreme Court,[110] but their importance is that they are used extensively in

[107] UNIDROIT, *Principles*, www.unidroit.org/wp-content/uploads/2021/06/Unidroit-Principles-2016-English-i.pdf.

[108] 1994 and 2004 (Professor Michael Furmston), 2010 (Professor Sir Roy Goode), 2016 (Sir Vivian Ramsay).

[109] Sir Roy Goode, *Creativity and Transnational Commercial Law: From Carchemish to Cape Town* (2021) 70 ICLQ 1.

[110] Lord Sumption in giving the judgment of the majority Supreme Court on a case as to the efficacy of a no oral modification clause, *Rock Advertising v MWB Business Exchange* [2018] UKSC 24 at para 13, where he referred to the UNIDROIT Principles and CISG as 'widely used codes' in addition to extensive citation of US authorities. Lord Briggs reached the same result by a narrower route.

arbitrations. Where arbitrators are from different legal systems, the principles provide a general statement of law applicable to transnational transactions, which is considered by many as far easier to ascertain than English commercial law. It is, however, soft law, not transnational law, and can only take effect through national law either by incorporation into a contract or as inspiration for courts or arbitrators when applying to a national legal system.[111]

Second is the 2001 *UNIDROIT Cape Town Convention on International Interests in Mobile Equipment* (such as aircraft and trains),[112] which has been adopted by eighty-eight nations. I mention it as it was an ambitious convention, not a model law. The lesson learnt from it appears for the future to be that UNIDROIT will, like UNCITRAL, also concentrate on model laws and engage with business at every stage. It is easier to get a model law agreed in this way and to get business to back its national implementation than proceeding by international convention.

Third are the *UNIDROIT Principles on Digital Assets and Private Law* published in May 2023.[113] The principles are not a model law. In phraseology commonly used in instruments of this type, principles are set out that, in phrases redolent of terms used to stress the advantages of

[111] See Beale at paragraphs 32–33 and 49–55. [112] And its protocols.

[113] UNIDROIT, *Principles on Digital Assets and Private Law*, www.unidroit.org/wp-content/uploads/2023/04/C.D.-102-6-Principles-on-Digital-Assets-and-Private-Law.pdf. English law has very powerful representation through Professor Louise Gullifer.

English commercial law, are designed to 'increase legal certainty and predictability' and are intended to act as 'guidance as to ways in which existing national law may need to be adapted in its application to digital assets' and as guidance 'to those involved in adjudicating disputes concerning digital assets, such as judges and arbitrators and to those involved in the transactions, such as practitioners and market participants'.

Unsurprisingly, digital assets have been the subject of much work in many different nations. In June 2023, the UK Law Commissions published its report[114] on digital assets aimed to ensure that the evolution of the markets in digital assets markets can readily use English commercial law. The Law Commission considered closely not only the work of UNIDROIT but also the views of the specialist judges in the UK, the UK Jurisdiction Taskforce, the American Law Institute and the Uniform Law Commissioners in the US and Scottish Emerging Technologies Committee.[115] The Law Commission's recommendation that there be a single statutory change to English law that would recognise digital assets as personal property and that the rest of the development of the law should be left to the judiciary was put before Parliament in 2025.

However, there is more to do as the very difficult issues relating to determining the relevant national system of law applicable to digital assets remains to be examined, given that the location of digital assets is not easy to

[114] Law Com 412.

[115] The Expert Reference Group on Digital Assets in Scots Private Law.

determine.[116] This is now the subject of joint work by HCCH and UNIDROIT,[117] as agreement on a generally accepted approach is essential.[118]

Fourth are the *ELI-UNIDROIT Model European Rules of Civil Procedure*,[119] which follow on from the *ALI-UNIDROIT Principles on Transnational Civil Procedure* (2004). It is important to draw attention to these, as one of the reasons why English commercial law has been so successful is the form of procedure adopted in England.[120] The ELI-UNIDROIT principles have been heavily influenced by English procedure and illustrate what is becoming evident in courts and arbitrations worldwide that the procedure developed in England is having a considerable influence in promoting efficient and effective dispute resolution worldwide – possibly yet another free rider.

116 The FMLC produced a report on this in 2018: *Distributed Leger Technology and the Governing Law.*

117 see: https://www.hcch.net/en/projects/legislative-projects/digital-tokens1.

118 The Law Commission has launched a project on this subject. The FMLC has, as mentioned, published its views in (June 2024) *Digital Assets – Governing Law and Jurisdiction*, https://fmlc.org/wp-content/uploads/2024/06/Report_Digital-Assets-Governing-Law-and-Jurisdiction.pdf.

119 ELI/UNIDROIT, *Model European Rules of Civil Procedure*, www.unidroit.org/english/principles/civilprocedure/eli-unidroit-rules/200925-eli-unidroit-rules-e.pdf. Also published in 2021, by Oxford University Press.

120 See Chapter 2 page <106>.

3.3.4.3 The Work of the European and American Law Institutes: Transnational Principles for the Data Economy

The transnational work of two private bodies – the American Law Institute to which I have referred in relation to restatements and the European Law Institute – is important. It is illustrated not only by the production of the joint ELI-UNIDROIT and ALI-UNIDROIT model rules on civil procedure but their jointly produced and published *Principles for a Data Economy*.[121] Much of the focus of governments on data has been on data privacy. However, at least as significant should be the economic importance of data, which requires the development of law that enables transactions to be governed by principles that take into account its specific characteristics – it is not property and is non-rivalrous. The principles published by the American Law Institute and the European Law Institute have engendered very considerable interest and influence not only in the US and EU but worldwide, including China. There are two important features of these principles: (1) the principles are designed to work within national legal systems (whether common law or civilian) by leaving issues such as remedies, privacy and consumer rights to national systems, and (2) they are intended to act as a guide for those in the market, those drafting contracts or legislation and those deciding disputes – in very much the same terms as the UNIDROIT principles on digital assets.

[121] American Law Institute/European Law Institute, December 2023.

The value of English engagement with these institutes can also be seen in the judicial leadership being given to developing principles for third party funding of litigation as a project of the European Law Institute.[122] Third party funding is a relatively new transnational business in which UK companies play a leading role. The issues that arise in its provision, whether in Asia, Australia or Europe are largely common, though solutions will have to be tailored. The leadership of this work is an example of judicial engagement that is, it is to be hoped, an example of what could and should be done.

3.3.4.4 Conclusion

In the short term, it is difficult to foresee parties to traditional commercial transactions moving away from their preference for a national law, such as English law, used transnationally. It has a body of learning that can be applied to most situations and is predicable.[123] However, for commerce based on digital assets and products, the question is much more open. The work and changes illustrated by these few examples of transnational instruments, model laws and principles raise the question as to how best English law should engage. I will return to this after considering the fifth option.

[122] Principles published on 9 October 2024, www.europeanlawinstitute.eu/fileadmin/user_upload/p_eli/Publications/ELI_Principles_Governing_the_Third_Party_Funding_of_Litigation.pdf.

[123] Lord Briggs (2019) *Mapping the Law in a Borderless World*, 33rd Sutan Azlan Shah Lecture, www.sultanazlanshah.com/pdf/2021/SAS_Lecture_33.pdf.

3.3.5 *Option 5: Pursuing Leadership of the Gradualist Role of the Courts in Developing Law That Is Used Transnationally*

3.3.5.1 The Commercial Court

Whichever of these options has the greatest attraction, it is the role of the English judges that is of central importance to ensuring English law is kept at the forefront and continued to be used as a dominant national system of law used transnationally. Its importance is reflected in the selection of English law as a system of national law to govern transnational contracts, as influencing the development of general principles adopted by bodies such as UNIDROIT and UNCITRAL and as promoting the selection of London and other UK venues for arbitration. As discussed in Chapter 2,[124] the judges developed the law whenever opportunity arose. For example, when the markets suffered disruptions, cases came to the judges for decision. In the second half of the twentieth century, it was successively cases on maritime law, then cases on grain, then cases on insurance and reinsurance that illustrate how activity in the markets drives litigation and the development of the law.

The Commercial Court has 125 years of history, but it must be recalled that there have been times during its history when it had little work.[125] Much has been done to ensure that the judges in the UK retain their international position. A good example is the move from the position that a

[124] See Chapter 2 at page <101>.

[125] See Lord Thomas *The Changing Business of the City of London.*

judge would not hear a case unless it arose in the context of a specific dispute; the test case procedure was adopted in 2015[126] to enable a case to be brought for judicial decision when an important issue had arisen in the market even though there was no actual dispute. The judges have throughout constantly strived to understand and keep pace with developments in trade, which I have described.

3.3.5.2 International Courts

The role of the UK judiciary must be seen, however, in the context of the very significant developments of the last twenty-five years. Most nations had courts that have in one way or another described themselves as commercial courts; their business in most nations has not been in any way comparable to that of the Commercial Court in London.

However, attempts have been made to emulate this more closely by the establishment of courts modelled on London,[127] as mentioned a little earlier. The Dubai International Financial Centre courts were established in 2004[128] and followed by Qatar in 2011, the Abu Dhabi

[126] Civil Procedure Rules PD 63A, paragraph 6.

[127] Georgios Dimitropoulos and Stavros Brekoulakis (eds.) (2022) *International Commercial Courts: The Future of Transnational Adjudication*, Cambridge University Press; Xandra Kramer and John Sorabji (eds.) (2019) *International Business Courts*, 11th International Publishing, Open Access is available; *Azmeh and Nicol on the Law and Practice of the QFC Civil and Commercial Court and Regulatory Tribunal*, 2025, Lexis Nexis. *DIFC Courts Practice* (Reed and Montague-Smith, eds.) 2nd edition 2024, Edward Elgar.

[128] DIFC Courts, www.difccourts.ae/.

Global Markets Courts[129] in 2016 and the Astana International Financial Centre Court[130] in Kazakhstan in 2018. Each was established as essentially common law courts often with a view to supporting the development of local financial and other commercial markets and free zones.

The view has been expressed that although these may be seen as an international manifestation of the quality of English law and of English judges and may serve local or regional needs without detriment to London, they might be in competition for dispute resolution business that might otherwise come to London.[131] In that respect in particular it is necessary to refer to Singapore and the courts being established within the EU.

Singapore has set about with some considerable success developing a commercial court within its court system, developing the Singapore International Arbitration Centre and establishing an International Commercial Court in 2015 with the stated aim of creating

> a trusted neutral forum to meet the growing demand for effective transnational dispute resolution through litigation due to Singapore's strategic location within Asia and the reputation of its world-class judiciary known for efficiency, competence and integrity.[132]

[129] ADGM Courts, www.adgm.com/adgm-courts.

[130] AIFC Court, https://court.aifc.kz/en; see also www.boomportaal.nl/tijdschrift/ELR/ELR-D-18-00027.

[131] By Lord Hodge (October 2022) *The Rule of Law, the Courts and the British Economy* [2023] LMCLQ 34 at 44.

[132] SICC, www.sicc.gov.sg/; Lucy Reed, John EC Brierley Memorial Lecture, *International Dispute Resolution Courts: Retreat or Advance*,

Its judges are largely drawn from the Singapore judiciary but additional judges have been appointed with that aim in mind and include not only judges from common law jurisdictions but judges from civilian traditions – France, Japan and China. Singapore has also been developing its contract law on the basis that it can, where appropriate, provide a clearer understanding of commercial realities than the English courts.[133] In cases of significance the judgments, particularly of its highest court, the Court of Appeal, often contain a thorough analysis of jurisprudence derived from many nations. Singapore also has the advantage that it is readily seen as a neutral and efficient court in a part of the world where those qualities might not always be discernible.

In the EU, international commercial courts have been established in Paris, Amsterdam and other cities. They are very much modelled on London, but without the addition of any non-national judges. By and large they hear cases in English. One advantage they have is their judgments are easily enforceable throughout Europe (an advantage the UK has lost as a result of Brexit and the blocking of the UK's request to join the Lugano Convention), but as can be seen from

11 September 2017, www.judiciary.gov.sg/docs/default-source/sicc-docs/news-and-articles/john-e-c-brierley-memorial-lecture—international-dispute-resolution-courts-retreat-or-advance-by-professor-lucy-reed_ea873680-6c44-403e-bfa1-802240fac519.pdf].

133 A recent example is *Charles Lim v David Wong* [2021] 2 SLR 153, [2021] SGCA 43, where the Singapore Court of Appeal did not follow the decision of the Supreme Court on no oral modification clauses in *Rock Advertising v MWB* referred to in note 110 in this chapter.

experience in other nations, some years are likely to elapse before these EU-based courts are likely to have significant business.

Features of commercial courts that most courts adopt are (1) procedures based on the UK model in case management and efficiency, (2) an activist approach to identifying the real issues in disputes, (3) the role of the judge as the decision-maker on all issues of fact rather than a court appointed expert, (4) the way witnesses are heard and examined, (5) the importance and style of advocacy, (6) the importance of effective enforcement of court judgments and orders, (7) the common law style of reasoned judgments and (8) the critical role of the Court Registry and Registrar in the running of the court, the scheduling of cases and relationships with the profession.

Unsurprisingly, England provides an excellent model, which is being emulated. The Qatar International Court has followed this model and is demonstrating the advantages of the way English law has developed. But with its judges drawn from many jurisdictions representing the common law and the civilian tradition as developed not only in Europe but elsewhere including those countries with an Islamic tradition, it may be easier to see greater convergence of national systems through the influence of judges from different traditions who sit together; this is increasingly shown in judgments.

If England's commercial law is to retain its position as the pre-eminent national system used for transnational commerce, the UK cannot allow itself to fall behind developments elsewhere. It cannot therefore at the present ignore the existence of an increasingly competitive market place between systems of substantive law and methods and places for dispute resolution; the English courts must show leadership in this respect as well as in the respects outlined in Option 2.

3.3.5.3 Development of Transnational Law by the Courts

In 2017[134] the UK led the establishment of the Standing International Forum of Commercial Courts with three aims:

- Business and markets will be better served if best practices are shared between courts and courts work together to keep pace with rapid commercial change.
- Courts acting together can make a stronger contribution to the rule of law than they can separately and through that contribute to stability and prosperity worldwide.
- Courts can better support developing jurisdictions (long encouraged by agencies such as the World Bank to enhance their attractiveness to investors by offering effective means for resolving commercial disputes).

One of the issues that is under active consideration is the development of principles of transnational commercial law, as

[134] The proposal was outlined by me in The Dubai International Financial Centre Academy of Law Lecture, 1 February 2016, *Commercial Justice in the Global Village: The Role of Commercial Courts*, at paragraphs 47–51, www.judiciary.uk/wp-content/uploads/2016/02/LCJ-commerical-justice-in-the-global-village-DIFC-Academy-of-Law-Lecture-February-2016.pdf. It was taken forward in 2017 with the support of Robn Knowles J, Williams Blair J, James Allsop CJ, Geoffrey Ma CJ, Sundaresh Menon CJ, Bart Katureebe CJ and Senior Judge Loretta Preska.

advocated by judges from some jurisdictions recently.[135] Some have described this as the new *Lex Mercatoria* or the new law merchant but this may not be an entirely apt term as it is not a call for a return to a *Lex Mercatoria* or for the new *Lex Mercatoria* as proposed by Professors Berthold Goldman, Clive Schmittoff and other legal scholars (as discussed in Chapter 2)[136] but to a system of law where the principles adopted are truly transnational (and not simply the application of general principles in a national system) and achieved by courts being influenced by each other. The aim, giving it a European label, is to achieve harmonisation through case law. It has been suggested by another proponent that a sure, though slow, way forward[137] is through judicial decisions influenced by the various instruments to which I have referred and other soft law instruments. This is a process applicable to the changes to transnational commerce consequent on digitalisation and the like. The changes, on analysis, give rise to the same legal solutions the law has always applied, though in different circumstances. Judges using case law and precedent are more likely to be able to respond more

[135] See, for example, Chief Justice Menon's lecture in Sydney in October 2022: 'SIFoCC playing its part as a cornerstone of a transnational system of commercial justice', www.judiciary.gov.sg/news-and-resources/news/news-details/chief-justice-sundaresh-menon-keynote-address-delivered-at-the-standing-international-forum-of-commercial-courts-2022 and Chief Justice Tom F. Bathurst (2015) *The Importance of Developing Commercial Law Systems*, Core Values of an Effective Judiciary, Singapore Academy of Law at pages 189–192.

[136] See Chapter 2 at page <139>.

[137] See Professor Ramberg's 4th Ole Lando Memorial Lecture at pages 9–10.

quickly and more adeptly than the legislator and in this the English courts must lead.

3.4 What Conclusions Can Be Drawn on the Future of the Law for Transnational Commerce?

Ultimately, it is difficult to see transnational commerce being operated on a basis where there is not either a de facto transnational law derived from a national system or an increasing volume of law that is transnational in the sense that it is broadly common to trading nations.

As I have outlined, English law faces significant competition, not the least from the fact that many of the traditional techniques of English commercial law are used by the courts of other nations. If England is to retain its position as providing the de facto transnational law or to have a significant influence on the development of transnational law, then it has to be transnational not only in outlook but in active participation. It has to be more cognisant of the merits of other systems. It must engage in the development of principles, model laws and other instruments. It must show more visibly that English law in its development is a national system that takes account of the importance of the development of transnational model laws, standard terms and principles and, just as in the nineteenth century and more recently in its examination of good faith, takes account of other national laws.

I have outlined some options in this chapter: (1) do nothing, (2) greater assistance to the courts, (3) the provision of an institutional structure for restatements, (4) a strategy for stronger engagement in the development of transnational law and (5) pursuing leadership of the gradualist role of the courts in developing law used transnationally. If the analysis I have put forward (or some of it) is accepted, doing nothing or muddling on with the other options is not viable. There needs to be the will, ability, vision and capacity to think radically. The provision of effective leadership within the UK to realise some or all of the options is an urgent task, as nothing can be achieved without effective leadership to take the necessary steps.

Leadership ensures that there is a clear sense of direction and clear coordination of the many different options mentioned in this chapter and other options that are available.[138] For example, the proper provision of comparative materials to the courts or information on scientific or market practice in cases where such are needed will not be possible without leadership. Similarly, leadership and a structure are essential if restatements are to have the necessary authority, in the way the American Law Institute has provided the leadership and the structure for over a century in the United States. It is not my task to suggest the way this should be established – my task has been simply to explain the necessity.

[138] In the 2016 Scarman Lecture, *Law Reform Now in 21st Century Britain: Brexit and Beyond*, I suggested that the Law Commission be given a specific role to keep English commercial law up to date with a wide remit to coordinate work in relation to the digital age and proper resources and independence from political whim, https://cloud-platform-e218f50a4812967ba1215eaecede923f.s3.amazonaws.com/uploads/sites/30/2017/06/lcj-speech-scarman-lecture-20170626.pdf.

Overall Conclusion

In looking at the needs of a nation for law and the needs of transnational commerce for law, what is required is an analysis of those needs to see how law can best meet those needs. That analysis of the needs and the way they can be met will differ over time as can be seen from the experience in Wales and in the development of English law in meeting the needs of transnational commerce. It is clear that different factors are at play. As a nation's laws are an important delineator of nationhood and the spirit of a nation, the study of Wales shows that it is principle that should govern the scope of the laws rather than political expediency and the desire to retain political power. In contrast, the law used for transnational commerce is based on pragmatism rather than principle and the need to use laws that support the interests of a nation in transnational commerce. However, no system can ever be complacent. It must consider both the adaptations needed so that it meets those changing needs and the way in which those adaptations are to be implemented so they achieve the necessary effect for the benefit of all the people of a nation.

INDEX

For EU product safety concerns, contact us at Calle de José Abascal, 56–1°, 28003 Madrid, Spain or eugpsr@cambridge.org.

www.ingramcontent.com/pod-product-compliance
Lightning Source LLC
LaVergne TN
LVHW010320220926
848484LV00004BB/814

* 9 7 8 1 0 0 9 6 2 7 8 3 2 *